NORTH AMERICAN CULTURES:

VALUES AND INSTITUTIONS IN CANADA AND THE UNITED STATES

BY

SEYMOUR MARTIN LIPSET

BORDERLANDS MONOGRAPH SERIES #3

BORDERLANDS

2056

The Borderlands Project

Americans and Canadians live together in North America as friends, allies, and partners in trade. The 5,000-mile border accommodates a diverse flow of people, commodities, and ideas. It is a paradox, but the sense of mutual security and amity afforded by a century's experience with the "undefended" border masks the border's complexity and importance. The open border is an immense asset that is routinely taken for granted. Consequently, the border relationship of Canada and the United States has not been adequately reflected in public policy discussions in the two countries.

The premise of the Borderlands Project is that North America runs more naturally north and south than east and west as specified by national boundaries, and that modern communication and efficient transportation help to blur distinctions between regional neighbors. While people living near the border pay allegiance to their respective sovereign authorities in Washington, D.C. and Ottawa, they sometimes have more in common with neighbors across the border than with their fellow citizens.

The Borderlands Project is meant to promote greater recognition and understanding of the status of the United States and Canada as border neighbors. It is a comprehensive study of transborder attributes undertaken by a multidisciplinary team of social science and humanities scholars from both sides of the border. The study will culminate in the publication of an important reference book for educators, government officials, business and civic leaders, journalists, and general readers in both countries. A series of monographs reporting on current borderlands research is also offered, as a record of scholarship in this cross-disciplinary area. The Borderlands Project constitutes a new set of lenses for seeing the two-way importance of the American-Canadian relationship. The project is designed to communicate the results of borderlands research to a growing audience in both countries.

The American-Canadian border provides a rare model of a social laboratory. Most of the eastern half is a natural water division between the two countries; the western half is an artificial surveyor's line. Which is the more real division between attitudes, values, and allegiances? In some cases, similarities (the pervasive impact of television, for instance) bring border neighbors closer together. In other cases, the similarities of some adjacent regions (for example, the reliance on basic industries such as farming or automaking) may produce competitive frustrations.

The American-Canadian Borderlands Project is not driven by ideological commitment; neither nationalist nor continentalist agendas have informed it. As a new set of lenses for policymakers, it is meant only to sharpen the images of reality formed by competition and cooperation between two industrial democracies in North America.

Acknowledgement

The Borderlands Project was initiated with financial support from the William H. Donner Foundation, Inc. Major funding was contributed as well by the Government of Canada through its Embassy in Washington D.C. The provincial governments of Québec and Saskatchewan have provided additional funds for research. To all of the above we express our sincere thanks for their significant contributions.

For additional information about the Borderlands Project contact:

The Canadian-American Center

Canada House, 154 College Avenue

University of Maine

Orono, ME 04469

Borderlands Monograph Series

The Borderlands Project is a research and compiling effort designed to produce a borderlands sourcebook for government officials, educators, and private-sector executives in both the United States and Canada. With more than 100 scholars involved in borderlands research, the project has received numerous manuscripts. In order to communicate research rapidly and to establish a borderlands dialogue, we have also inaugurated a Borderlands Monograph Series. Each monograph is a major statement of current work in some aspect of American-Canadian relations, and, as a whole, the series will stand as a record of the depth and diversity of borderlands research, as applied to the relationship between Canada and the United States.

Editors

Alan Artibise (University of British Columbia)

Victor Konrad (University of Maine)

Peter Kresl (Bucknell University)

Robert Lecker (McGill University)

Lauren McKinsey (Montana State University)

About the Author

Professor Seymour Martin Lipset, Caroline S.G. Munro Professor of Political Science, Professor of Sociology, Stanford University, and Senior Fellow, Hoover Institution, Stanford University, is a founder of the Comparative School of Political and Sociological Analysis. His work has pioneered the development of political national identities. Professor Lipset's research activities have kept him at the forefront of Canadian studies, particularly in the area of Canada's role in the international environment. His most recent book, *Continental Divide: The Values and Institutions of the United States and Canada,* will be published in March 1990, by Routledge. The book will appear simultaneously in the United States, Canada, and Great Britain.

North American Cultures: Values and Institutions in Canada and the United States

Seymour Martin Lipset

The debate that has occurred on a wide scale in Canada and on a limited one in the United States concerning the Free Trade Agreement between the two countries has returned the subjects of national identity and values to the centers of attention north of the border.[1] Many English-speaking Canadian intellectuals have argued that, although North American countries have differed greatly from the postfeudal European nations, Canada bears more of a resemblance to Britain and France than does the United States.[2] As the controversy over the Free Trade Agreement has developed, nationalist intellectuals have expressed fear that greater economic integration in North America will lead to the extinction of English-speaking Canada as a separate culture and, ultimately, as part of an independent nation. They have suggested that, in order to compete within a North American common market, Canada and her provinces will have to give up many of the social-welfare and public-benefit policies that have distinguished them as polities more socially democratic than the United States. Although the focus of these arguments has recently been on the effects of free trade, such criticisms of American influence long predate the drafting of the agreement.

No corresponding anxieties have been voiced by Americans. There has, of course, been considerable debate about the impact of the Free Trade Agreement on the American economy. But those involved in American cultural activities have not reacted to the possibility of increased competition from their Canadian compeers, or to the potential inherent in a larger cultural market. And since few in the United States have seriously considered the possibility that the agreement could eventually lead to their incorporation into a common North American polity, there has been no analysis of the possible effects of Canadian participation in one political system with the United States.

This work will focus on the sources and nature of the cultural and

1

value differences between the two countries. In it, I try to interpret aspects of North American cultures as reflections of the key organizing principles that derive from their varying histories and ecologies.[3] The central argument of this essay is that Canada has been a more class-aware, elitist, law-abiding, statist, collectivity-oriented, and particularistic (group-oriented) society than the United States,[4] and that these fundamental distinctions stem in large part from the defining event that gave birth to both countries, the American Revolution, and from the diverse ecologies flowing from the division of British North America. The social effects of this division have been subsequently reflected in, and reinforced by, variations in literature, religious traditions, political and legal institutions, and socio-economic structures that have been created in each country.

Any effort to analyze the cultures or values of nations confronts the fact that statements about them are necessarily made in a comparative context. Thus, the statement that a national value system is egalitarian does not imply the absence of differences of power, income, wealth, or status. Rather, it means that, from a comparative perspective, nations classified as egalitarian *tend* to place more emphasis on universalistic criteria in judging others, and tend to de-emphasize the institutionalization of hierarchical differences.

What appear as significant differences when viewed through one lens may seem to be minor variations viewed through another. For example, Louis Hartz has argued that Canada, the United States, and other countries settled by groups emigrating from Europe, are all "fragment cultures" that lacked the privileged aristocratic class and its institutions that were found in the European "whole." Over time, the absence of a traditional right transmuted the original liberal or radical doctrines into conservative dogmas of the "fragment." It is impossible to build an ideological left in such cultures because there is no hereditary aristocracy against which to rebel, and because the philosophical bases on which an ideological left might be founded are already institutionalized as part of the received liberal and radical tradition of the society.[5]

Hence, for Hartz, the American Revolution is not a watershed event marking a radical distinction between the value system developing in postrevolutionary America and that emerging in counterrevolutionary Canada. Although he does note that "The democratic spirit in English Canada is etched with a Tory streak coming out of the American Revolution," the differences between the two countries are less significant to him than the traits common to both that set them off from European societies.[6] By contrast, the perspective emphasized here sees a greater degree of continuity between the communitarian and elitist aspects of monarchical Britain and the character of Canadian value orientations

2

than Hartz's analysis suggests.

It is precisely because Canada and the United States have so much in common that they permit the student to gain insights into the factors that cause variations. I strongly support Robin Winks in his view that

> the historian [or social science analyst] of the United States who is ignorant of Canadian history [society] is ignorant of his own history [society]. . . . In short, the reason Americans should study Canadian history [society and politics] is to learn more about themselves.[7]

The converse, of course, holds for Canadians, although they need much less urging on the subject than Americans.

The Background

Given the contrasts between the American historical experience and the Canadian, it is not surprising that the peoples of the two countries formed their self-conceptions in disparate ways. The emphases on individualism and achievement by the American colonists were important motivating forces in the launching of the American Revolution, and were embodied in the Declaration of Independence. The manifestation of such attitudes in this founding event, and their crystallization in a historical document, provided a basis for their reinforcement and encouragement in what became a populist format throughout subsequent American history. The ideology of the American Revolution has provided a raison d'être for the republic, explaining why the United States came into being and what it means to be American. Canada, by contrast, has continued to debate her self-conception up to the present. The country began as the part of British North America that did not support the Revolution, and Canadians have continued to define themselves by reference to what they are not—American—rather than in terms of their own national history and tradition. There is no ideology of "Canadianism," comparable to "Americanism."

By the end of the first decade of the American republic, the conservative, more elitist right-wing party—the Federalists—was declining, and ultimately it disappeared. The Jeffersonian Democrats, who were more egalitarian and more supportive of the French Revolution, came to power and remained dominant. Succeeding opponents of the Democratic party, the Whigs and the Republicans, chose names that identified them with the revolutionary and Jeffersonian traditions. The United States remained through the nineteenth and early twentieth centuries the extreme example of a classically liberal or Lockean society that rejected the assumptions of the alliance of throne and altar, of ascriptive

3

elitism, or mercantilism, of noblesse oblige, or communitarianism.

Both major Canadian linguistic groups sought to preserve their values and cultures by reacting against liberal revolution. English-speaking Canada exists because she rejected the Declaration of Independence; French-speaking Canada, largely under the leadership of Catholic clerics, isolated herself from the anticlerical democratic values of the French Revolution.[8] After 1783 and 1789, the leaders of both cultures consciously attempted to create a conservative, monarchical, and ecclesiastical society in North America.

If early American history can be seen as a triumph of the more leftist Jeffersonian-Jacksonian tendencies, many Canadian historians and sociologists have emphasized that the conservative forces continued to win out north of the border until late in the twentieth century.[9] Canada, of course, was no more politically homogeneous than the United States, but its nineteenth-century populist reform wings lost out while the equivalent groups in the United States were winning. Many of these more populist, more democratic, and more egalitarian groups—such as those involved in the Mackenzie and Papineau rebellions—viewed the United States in positive terms. They were in effect saying "our ancestors made a mistake." Frank Underhill sums up this history:

> Our forefathers made the great refusal in 1776 when they declined to join the revolting American colonies. They made it again in 1812 when they repelled the American invasions. They made it again in 1837 when they rejected a revolution motivated by ideals of Jacksonian democracy, and opted for a staid moderate respectable British Whiggism which they called "Responsible Government." They made it once more in 1867 when the separate British colonies joined to set up a new nationality in order to preempt the northern half of the continent from American expansion. . . . In fact, it would be hard to overestimate the amount of energy we have devoted to this cause.[10]

This sequence is understandable given the legitimation of conservatism in Canada flowing from the rejections of the liberal American and French revolutions, and from patterns of emigration and immigration that reinforced right-wing trends. These include the departure of bourgeois, rationalist, and Huguenot elements from Quebec after the British Conquest, and the arrival of conservative priests who fled France in reaction to adverse events there. In the English-speaking areas, most pro-Revolution Congregational clergy moved to New England, and an estimated fifty thousand Loyalists—including many Anglican priests—crossed the new border in the opposite direction.

Unlike the United States, Canada evolved gradually as an independent nation. The unification of the provinces of British North America into the Dominion of Canada in 1867 was not an act in defiance of the British Crown; instead, it reflected the fact that the British had sought for some decades to give up much of their responsibility for the North American territories, while retaining them as part of the British Empire. The leaders of the confederation movement were mainly Conservatives who preferred strong ties with Great Britain. As William Stahl reports, "Devotion to the Crown was the one element that all the Fathers of Confederation shared."[11]

The link with Britain has persisted into the present day and has, to some extent, inhibited the emergence of a distinctive Canadian identity. Until 1982, the constitution of the Canadian confederation was the British North America Act, proclaimed by the queen. From its passage in 1867 until the adoption of the Constitution Act of 1982, Canadians had to petition the overseas House of Commons for any amendment to the act. Before 1949, the ultimate court of appeals for Canada was the Privy Council of Great Britain. Canadian lawyers had to go to London to argue constitutional cases as well as other kinds of appeals. The 1978 Immigration Act gave Canadians a distinct citizenship for the first time. The Maple Leaf only became the national flag in 1965, and not until 1980 did "O Canada" replace "God Save the Queen" as the national anthem.

A more enduring British influence has been Toryism, which took root, survived, and deeply influenced Canadian culture and policies:

> Toryism was not reducible simply to an economic doctrine masquerading as a philosophy. . . . The emphasis on *control* of the processes of national development, the element of the collective will of the dominant class expressed through the public institutions of the state, while seemingly anachronistic in an increasingly laissez-faire Britain, was crucially relevant to a thinly settled frontier colony struggling on the fringes of a growing economic and political power to the south.[12]

Some of the modern scholars who also see Canada as a more British- or European-type conservative society stress that the values inherent in monarchically rooted Tory conservatism give rise in the modern world to support for social-democratic redistribution and welfare policies.[13] Gad Horowitz has noted that "socialism has *more* in common with toryism than with [classic] liberalism for liberalism is possessive individualism, while socialism and toryism are variants of collectivism."[14] A dominant laissez-faire Lockean tradition is antithetical to such programs. Other analysts, while agreeing that Canadian values and behavior

5

are different from American, point to the need to consider also the causal impact of variations in the ecology, demography, and economy of the two nations. Canada controls an area that, though larger than the United States, is much less hospitable to human habitation in terms of climate and resources. Her size and weaker population base have reinforced the Tory-statist tradition of direct government involvement in the economy, since it has been necessary to provide services for which sufficient private capital or a profitable market has not been available.[15] In addition to greater state intervention, extensive bureaucratic organizations and less individual enterprise developed in Canada. As S.D. Clark notes, south of the border, the antistatist emphasis subsumed in the classically liberal revolutionary ideology was not challenged by the need to call upon the state to intervene economically to protect the nation's independence against a powerful neighbor.[16]

A comparison of the frontier experiences of the two countries encapsulates the ways in which values and structural factors have interacted to produce different outcomes. Inasmuch as Canada had to be on constant guard against the expansionist tendencies of the United States, she could not leave her frontier communities unprotected or autonomous. "It was in the established tradition of British North America that the power of the civil authority should operate well in advance of the spread of settlement."[17] In the United States, by contrast, the Atlantic Ocean provided an effective barrier against the major locus of perceived threat—Britain—which helped sustain the American ideological commitment to a weak state that, until the post-World War II era, did not have to maintain extensive military forces.

Law and order in the form of the centrally controlled Northwest Mounted Police moved into the Canadian frontier before, and along with, the settlers. This contributed to a deeper respect for the institutions of law and order on the Canadian frontier than on the American, thus undermining the development of individualism and disrespect for authority that has been more characteristic of the United States.

Formative national events and images, revolution and counter-revolution, continued to affect the way the two countries regarded themselves into the twentieth century.[18] However, Canadians have not been unanimous in their view of themselves or their neighbor. One study of Canadian attitudes during the 1920s documents the ways in which such judgments varied along political lines.[19] Conservatives stressed the Tory belief in the use of the state to foster noblesse-oblige objectives, and were especially deprecating about egalitarianism and democracy in the United States.[20] They wished to maintain the British tie and even to strengthen the link to the empire. On the other hand, many Liberals were continentalists, adhering to traditions that were closer to those of the Americans. At the same time, leftists, then as later, worried about an American takeover of Canada. The radicals tended to be more nationalistic in their sentiments. Similar divisions are observable today.

Values and structures do change. Canada and the United States have followed the general tendencies in most Western nations toward a greater acceptance of communitarian welfare and egalitarian standards, a decline in religious commitment, an increase in educational attainment, a greater role for government, and a shift in the composition of the economy from primary and secondary industries toward tertiary service and high-tech and information-based ones, as well as population movement from rural to urban areas. These structural changes, along with the diffusion of values through rapid transportation and almost instantaneous communication, seem to be producing a common Western culture. Yet many national differences persist, some in weaker form, while others emerge, as the discussion that follows will illustrate. As Richard Gwyn has stated, Canadians have become

> a quite distinct kind of North American. ... utterly unalike [those in the United States] in their political cultures so that they are as distinct from each other as are the Germans from the French, say, even though both are Europeans just as Canadians and Americans are both North Americans.[21]

The debate as to the sources and nature of the differences continues. The cultural (value-oriented) and structuralist approaches are not mutually exclusive. For example, Canada's foremost economic historian, Harold Innis, though clearly emphasizing structural factors in his discussion of cross-national variations, also notes the importance of the "essentially counter-revolutionary traditions, represented by the United Empire Loyalists and by the Church in French Canada, which escaped the influences of the French Revolution."[22] In turning now to a systematic comparison of a number of facets of the two societies, including literature, religion, economy, law and crime, and center-periphery relations, I shall continue to observe this mutual interaction between the values predominant in the two nations and the institutions that both reflect and shape them.

Literature and Myths

Northrop Frye has argued that "A culture founded on a revolutionary tradition, like that of the United States, is bound to show very different assumptions and imaginative patterns from those of a culture that rejects or distrusts revolution."[23] And, indeed, many literary critics

7

have pursued the revolution-counterrevolution theme in their comparative analyses of North American literatures. For example, Margaret Atwood has suggested that the central symbol for America is "The Frontier," which "suggests a place that is *new*, where the old order can be discarded." The comparable image in Canadian writing, based on numerous examples of its appearance in French and English Canadian literature, is "Survival, *la Survivance*," "hanging on, staying alive." Atwood notes the continued Canadian concern with Canada: does it exist?; what is Canadian identity?; do we have an identity?; and so on. As she puts it, "Canadians are forever taking the national pulse like doctors at a sickbed: the aim is not to see whether the patient will live well but simply whether he will live at all."[24]

Like others, Atwood stresses the differences in the way the two societies look at authority, and argues that Canadians, unlike Americans, do not see authority or government as enemies. Rebels or revolutionists are not heroes in Canadian literature.[25] Atwood illustrates her general theme by looking at the different ways in which the family is treated in the literature of the two countries. She notes that "In American literature the family is something the hero must repudiate and leave; it is a structure he rebels against, thereby defining his own freedom, his own Frontier. . . . The family . . . is something you come from and get rid of." Canadian novels, however, treat the family quite differently: "if in America it's a skin you shed, then in Canada it's a trap in which you're caught."[26]

Russell Brown agrees that the variations in national literature stem from "crucial differences between American and Canadian societies," those related to their diverse political origins: "What is important . . . is not so much the effect of the revolution [or its lack] on the day-to-day life of individuals in the two countries, it is rather the myths and the psychic consequences of founding a country on revolution or on the rejection of revolution."[27] Thus, south of the border, novels emphasize rejection of the father by the sons, a rejection parallel to that of the British king by the Americans: that is to say, American novels are Oedipal.[28]

Canadian writing, however, is quite different in its treatment of the father, reflecting differences in "the way the nation first conceived of itself in relation to its country . . . of origin, its fatherland."[29] Brown suggests that there is an alternative to Oedipus in Greek literature and myth, Telemachus, whose story is reflected in a great deal of Canadian writing. Telemachus's problem is that "the king, his father, has departed, has left him to grow up fatherless in his mother's home for reasons he cannot fully grasp, or at any rate experientially comprehend." Hence, he sets out at the beginning of the *Odyssey* to find his father, trying to discover the events that took him away from his son.[30] He cites various Canadian novels as reflecting the Telemachus syndrome, including Hugh MacLennan's *Each Man's Son,* Robert Kroetsch's *Badlands,* and Margaret Laurence's *Diviners.*

Mary Jean Green, a student of Quebec literature, agrees that the counterrevolutionary theme is important in forming Canada's culture, but suggests that the family-tension myth north of the border reflects the stresses of the mother-daughter relationship rather than the father-son one. According to Freudian analysis, the son fights the father, but the daughter "though . . . initially overcome by hostility . . . can never fully abandon her very strong feelings of attachment and continuity with the mother." Hence, "the importance accorded mother-daughter interaction in the ideological context of Quebec," and anglophone Canada as well. The theme of many recent Canadian novels in both French and English has been the feminine one "of rejection and reconciliation," not the more masculine theme of the sharp break.[31]

Another theme related to the effects of the counterrevolutionary origins of Canada has been suggested by novelist Hugh MacLennan. He contends that Canadian culture reflects the fact that its three founding nationalities, the English, the French, and the Scots, are defeated peoples: the English by the Americans, and the French and the Jacobite Scots who settled Nova Scotia by the English.[32] In line with this thesis, Scott Symons points out that major Canadian writers, such as Hubert Aquin, Marie-Claire Blais, and Leonard Cohen, have written "for a society whose bravest souls have been 'beautiful losers' "(the title of a novel by Cohen.)[33] Atwood notes that the heroes of Canadian novels "survive, but just barely; they are born losers" failing "to do anything but keep alive."[34] These literary images reach out to a broader public. In its New Year's issue for 1986, the Canadian monthly, *Saturday Night,* presented a front cover headed in large type: "BEAUTIFUL LOSERS—A Canadian Tradition." The inside story noted that Canada is "Not quite a country where dreams come true, not exactly a land where the good guys always win. . . . Losses . . . marked our steady passage. Partaking of a [long] tradition . . . Canadians frequently came back from their adventures empty-handed."[35]

A similar point has been made about English Canadian motion pictures. Robert Fothergill asked in 1973, "Does the blight on male characters in our films—our fantasies—genuinely reflect a sense of limitation and inadequacy experienced half-consciously by Canadians in their real lives"; does it reflect a "return to a defeatist fantasy"?[36] More than a decade later, Geoff Pevere finds that Fothergill's thesis helps "to account for the losers roaming around Canadian films." He also notes the persistent proliferation of outsiders as heroes in Canadian movies. . . . And, unlike the romantic American version of the outlaw as a transcendent figure whose nowhereness permits him an invulnerable omnipotence and godlike heroism, the Canadian outcast is defined by his being less and not greater than those communities that have rejected him.[37]

The differences in themes, particularly between the two North American national literatures, appear to be declining. A.J.M. Smith and Ronald Sutherland call attention to the effects of a new nationalism north of the border that is producing more radical writing. But ironically, as Sutherland points out, these changes are making Canada and her fiction more American, since they involve a greater emphasis on values such as national pride, self-reliance, individualism, independence, and self-confidence.[38] However, it may be argued that these shifts, while reducing some traditional differences, have enhanced others. The new nationalism, often linked, when manifested among intellectuals, to socialism and Toryism, seeks to resist takeover of Canada's economy and increased cultural and media influence by Americans, and its weapon in so doing is the traditional Canadian remedy of state intervention.

Religion

Harold Innis may have encapsulated the different religious traditions in Canada and the United States when he wrote that "A counter-revolutionary tradition implies an emphasis on ecclesiasticism."[39] Historically, the majority of Canadians have adhered to the Roman Catholic or Anglican churches,[40] both of which are hierarchically organized and, until recently, had a strong relationship to the state. Canada has

> never succeeded in drawing with any precision a line between areas in which the state has a legitimate interest and those that ought to be left to the voluntary activities of the churches. . . . [F]ew Canadians find "the separation of church and state" an acceptable description either of their situation or of their ideal for it.[41]

Both the Roman Catholic church and the Church of England, in return for government support, endorsed the established political and social orders up to the post-World War II era. Hence one found mutually reinforcing conservative forces at the summits of the class, church, and political structures.[42] While efforts to sustain church establishment ultimately failed in Canada, state support of religious institutions, particularly schools, continues in all provinces except British Columbia.[43]

10

On the other hand, the American tradition and law place more emphasis on separation of church and state than do the Canadian. A large majority of Americans have adhered to the more individualist nonconformist Protestant sects, which had opposed the established state church in England. These denominations have a congregational structure, and promote the concept of a personal relationship with God. In a speech to Parliament, Edmund Burke tried to explain the motives and behavior of the American colonists at the time of the Revolution by saying that their religious beliefs made them the Protestants of Protestantism, the dissenters of dissent, the individualists par excellence.[44] Tocqueville pointed out that all American denominations were minorities, and hence had an interest in liberty and a weak state.[45]

Just as religious practices and institutions can reinforce general value orientations prevalent in a national community, so too can the latter influence the former, as is demonstrated in Kenneth Westhues's comparative study of the Catholic church in both countries. Westhues suggests that there has been an "acceptance by the American Catholic church of the role of voluntary association . . . as the most it could hope for."[46] Thus, the Catholic church in the United States has taken on many of the characteristics of Protestantism, including a strong emphasis on individual morality.[47] As a result, the Vatican has frowned on the American church and has, in fact, not treated it as well as the Canadian affiliate. This is reflected in a lower ratio of honors, saints, and cardinals to the Catholic population in the United States as compared to the Catholic population in Canada. The tension between the Vatican and the American Catholic church is a result of the difference "between that world-view, espoused by the American state, which takes the individual as the basic reality of social life, and the church's world-view, which defines the group as primary."[48]

The American voluntaristic and sectarian religious traditions have encouraged the rise of many new denominations—such as the Mormons, Seventh Day Adventists, Christian Scientists, and Jehovah's Witnesses—in the United States while in Canada the tradition has been much less theologically fecund.[49] Harry Hiller argues that religious innovation north of the border has been more limited "because of the presence of institutional controls in which alliances between the state and established religious institutions deliberately sought to discourage religious experimentation."[50] In the United States, by contrast, religion "is marketed with the flair and aggressiveness of a 'hot' commercial commodity."[51]

Religion in both countries has become more secularized in tandem with increased urbanization and education. Canadian Catholicism, particularly in Quebec, has modified the nature of its corporatist commitment from a link to agrarian and elitist anti-industrial values to a tie with leftist socialist beliefs. Public-opinion research suggests that francophone Catholics have given up much of their commitment to Jansenist puritanical values, particularly as they affect sexual behavior and family size.

This secularizing trend has been less noticeable in the United States, according to survey data collected in the two countries. Comparable questions bearing on religion have been asked over the years by the Gallup Poll, questions concerning the subjects' belief in God and church attendance. Gallup has reported for some time that around 95 to 96 percent of Americans and 86 to 87 percent of Canadians are believers. Figures for 1988 show that 40 percent of Americans and 32 percent of Canadians indicate they had been to a "church or synagogue in the last seven days." Catholics in both countries show a higher rate of attendance than Protestants, about 15 percent more on average. Since the proportion of Catholics is greater in Canada, the national differences increase when religion is held constant.

The published results of a survey by CARA (Center for Applied Research in the Apostolate), carried out by the Gallup Poll in the two countries, differentiates the responses of English and French Canadians, but not by religious affiliation.[52] These results show, among other things, that Americans are more religious and more moralistic than Canadians. When asked to respond to the question, "How important is God in your life?" on a ten-point scale (one meaning not at all; and ten, very important), 59 percent of the Americans placed themselves at nine or ten; as opposed to 44 percent of the English Canadians and 47 percent of the French Canadians. Close to two-thirds of the Americans, 65 percent, said they believe "there is a personal God," compared to 49 percent of the English Canadians and 56 percent of the French Canadians.

Americans far outnumbered Canadians in expressing fundamentalist beliefs, with anglophones more likely to hold such views than francophones. Thus, when asked whether they believed in the devil, 66 percent of Americans said yes, as did 46 percent of English Canadians, compared with only 25 percent of French Canadians. The responses to questions about belief in hell were similar: 67 percent for the Americans, 45 percent for the English Canadians, and 22 percent for the French Canadians. The overwhelming majority of Americans, 84 percent, said they believed in the existence of heaven, as did 73 percent of the English Canadians and 58 percent of the French Canadians. Almost three-quarters, 71 percent, of Americans expressed belief in life after death, compared to 61 percent of the English and 63 percent of the French Canadians.

Congruent with the variation in religious practice and belief, the

CARA-Gallup data also indicate that Americans are more puritanical than Canadians, with francophones the most tolerant with respect to sexual behavior. Nineteen percent of the French Canadians agreed that "marriage is an outdated institution," as did 11 percent of the English Canadians and 7 percent of the Americans. When asked the question, "If a woman wants to have a child as a single parent but she doesn't want to have a stable relationship with a man, do you approve or disapprove?" Americans voiced the highest rate of disapproval—58 percent, compared to 53 percent for Canadian anglophones and 34 percent for the francophones. A similar pattern is reflected in replies to the question—"If someone says that sexual activity cannot entirely be left up to individual choice, there have to be moral rules to which everyone adheres, do you tend to agree or disagree?" A small majority, 51 percent, of Americans agreed, as did 49 percent of the English Canadians but only 34 percent of the French Canadians.

Much of organized Christendom has changed its secular orientation in the postwar decades. The traditionally established churches have become the foremost exponents of "liberation theology," as many in the churches have turned towards a left-wing anticapitalist and communitarian position. Both Canadian and American Catholicism have moved to the left, but the Canadian church has gone further. In 1988, the American socialist magazine *Dissent* published a statement of the Canadian bishops on social policy because the editors correctly viewed it as basically socialist.[53] The parallel document by the American bishops is much more moderate. The United Church of Canada has endorsed the statement issued by the hierarchy of their Catholic co-nationals. Unlike the American sects, the United Church "has been a major force in the last 30 years in pressing for increased spending on social welfare programs and for the rights of prisoners, workers and Canada's native people."[54] Clearly the different religious traditions of the two countries help to explain much of their varying secular behaviors and beliefs.

Law and Deviance

Many of the efforts to distinguish Canada and the United States have emphasized the greater respect for law, and for those who uphold it, north of the border. These variations are linked to the historical emphasis on the rights and obligations of the community as compared to those of the individual. The concern of Canada's Fathers of Confederation with "Peace, Order, and Good Government" implies control of, and protection for the society. The parallel stress by America's Founding Fathers on "Life, Liberty, and the Pursuit of Happiness" suggests upholding the rights of the individual. The American commitment to personal rights, including those of political dissidents and people accused of crimes, is inherent in the "due process" model, which involves various legal inhibitions on the power of the police and prosecutors. The "crime control" model, more evident in Canada and Europe, emphasizes the maintenance of law and order, and is less protective of the rights of the accused and of individuals generally.[55]

The lesser respect for the law, for the rules of the game, in the United States may be viewed as inherent in a system in which egalitarianism is strongly valued and in which diffuse elitism is lacking. Generalized deference is not accorded to those at the top in the United States; therefore there is a greater propensity to redefine or ignore the rules. While Canadians incline toward the use of lawful and institutionalized means for altering regulations that they believe are unjust, Americans seem more disposed to employ informal and often extralegal means to correct what they perceive as wrong.

The greater lawlessness and corruption in the United States may also be attributed in part to a greater emphasis on achievement. As Robert Merton has noted, achievement orientation means that "The moral mandate to achieve success thus exerts pressure to succeed, by fair means if possible and by foul means if necessary."[56] This suggests that, since Americans are more likely than their Canadian neighbors to be concerned with the achievement of *ends*—particularly pecuniary success—they will be less concerned with the use of the socially appropriate *means*. Hence we should expect a higher incidence of deviations from conventional norms south of the forty-ninth parallel.

That Canadians and Americans vary in this way is demonstrated strikingly in the aggregate differences between the two with respect to crime rates for major offenses.[57] Americans are much more prone than Canadians to commit violent offenses such as murder, robbery, and rape, and to be arrested for the use of serious illegal drugs such as opiates and cocaine. For example, in 1987, the murder rate for Canada was 2.5 per 100,000 population; for the United States it was 8.3.[58] The United States not only has a much higher rate of homocide than Canada but it also has a considerably higher level of political violence. Data reported in the *World Handbook of Political and Social Indicators* show that Canadians were much less likely than Americans to engage in protest demonstrations or riots between 1948 and 1977. Although the American population outnumbers the Canadian by about ten to one, the ratios for political protest activities have been from two to four times as large, that is ranging from twenty to one to forty to one.[59]

The lower rates of crime and violence in Canada are accompanied by greater respect for police and a higher level of support for gun-control legislation. In the early eighties, the comparative value surveys conducted by Gallup for CARA found more Canadians (86 percent) than Americans (76 percent) voicing a great deal of confidence in the police.[60] Variations in attitudes toward the legal system were similar: 63 percent of Canadians had positive feelings about it, compared to 51 percent of Americans. On this question, however, Canadian francophones revealed more confidence (72 percent) than anglophones (59 percent).

In the United States, gun ownership has been regarded as a right linked to a constitutional guarantee established to protect citizens against the state. Canadian policy has been more restrictive, based on the belief that "ownership of offensive weapons or guns is a privilege, not a right."[61] Gallup surveys conducted in 1975 showed 83 percent of Canadians indicating support for "a law which would require a person to obtain a police permit before he or she could buy a gun," compared to 67 percent of Americans.[62] Canadian gun laws were tightened considerably in 1976. Handgun permits are only issued "after an investigation to determine the crime-free status and sanity of the applicant." A representative of the Justice Department noted in 1986 that "It is almost impossible to get a permit to carry a handgun."[63]

Although the cross-national behavioral and attitudinal variations with respect to law and crime have continued to the present, Canada has been involved during the 1980s in a process of changing her fundamental rules in what have been described as American and due-process directions. The adoption of a comprehensive Charter of Rights and Freedoms in the new Constitution of 1982 was designed to create a basis, absent from the British North America Act, for judicial intervention to protect individual rights and civil liberties. Canadian courts have actively begun to practice the dictates of the charter.

While these changes are very important, it is doubtful that they have completely eliminated the differences in legal cultures. Canadian courts have been more respectful than American ones of the rest of the political system. In interpreting the "judicial deference to legislative judgment" in the first years of the charter, F.L. Morton and Leslie Pal suggest that this pattern "reflects the continued influence of the tradition of judicial self-restraint engendered by over a century of Canada's unique form of parliamentary supremacy."[64]

Furthermore, the charter is not the American Bill of Rights. While placing many comparable restrictions on government action, it still is not as protective of individuals accused of crime. As Edgar Friedenberg has noted:

The American Bill of Rights provides no person shall "for the same offense be twice put in jeopardy of life or limb." A similar

15

provision under Section 10(h) of the Canadian Charter of Rights and Freedoms is made ineffective in preventing what an American court would call "double jeopardy" by the inclusion of the word "finally"—"finally acquitted," "finally found guilty" —since the process is not considered final till the crown has exhausted its right to appeal [an acquittal] which, under American law, it wouldn't have in the first place.[65]

Other differences include the fact that the charter "does not protect generally the right to refuse to answer a question . . . on the basis of possible self-incrimination," and that defendants have a right to a jury trial only in cases where the maximum sentence "is at least five years."[66] Property rights are also under less constitutional protection in Canada than in the United States. As John Mercer and Michael Goldberg note, in the charter,

> property rights (as distinct from human rights) were explicitly not protected. . . . Such a state of affairs would be unacceptable in the United States where individual rights and particularly those related to personal and real property are sacrosanct.[67]

Instead of insisting, like the Bill of Rights, on "due process of law," the charter refers to "principles of fundamental justice," under which basic individual rights are assured. It also states, "these rights in the charter now enjoy a greatly enhanced legal status," and are subject to such "reasonable limit[s]" as can be "demonstrably justified in a free and democratic society." The charter's authors assumed that Parliament would be able to define "reasonable limits."[68] The Canadian Constitution also provides that Parliament or a provincial legislature may opt out of constitutional restrictions by inserting into a law a provision that it may operate "notwithstanding" the relevant sections of the charter.

> The only rights which cannot be overridden are the "democratic rights," "mobility rights," "minority language education rights," rights associated with the equal status of French and English in some parts of Canada, and in an interpretation clause providing that rights in the *Charter* are guaranteed equally to male and female persons.[69]

If Canadian law under the charter is somewhat more limited in its protection of individual rights than American law, it retains its traditional emphasis on collective rights. The 1867 Constitution had provisions protecting specific linguistic and religious minorities. The charter does protect many individual rights, but "The collective rights of minorities . . . . in particular language rights, will continue to enjoy pre-eminence."[70]

16

These include aboriginal rights and rights to sexual equality. The charter also authorizes affirmative-action programs. And, although individual rights may be overridden by Parliament or provincial legislatures, group rights may not. Thus, as José Woehrling concludes, the Canadian Constitution still reflects "a value system in which certain collective rights are of central importance."[71]

The Economy

Canada and the United States have been among the wealthiest and most productive nations in the world during this century. As of 1986, in terms of purchasing-power parities, the GDP per head for the United States was U.S. $17,360, while Canada was second among OECD countries at U.S. $15,910.[72] Not surprisingly, analyses of the varying levels of economic success in Canada and the United States can be distinguished by considering whether each of the two countries stresses structural or cultural factors.

The structural explanation of North American affluence emphasizes the advantages possessed by settlers occupying a continent open to development, with enormous agricultural, animal, and mineral resources. Within this shared context, the greater size of the American market has given business in the United States a considerable advantage compared to that in Canada. Canada has thus needed government capital and other assistance to establish and maintain the services and industries necessary for survival in a large country with a relatively small population.

The cultural interpretation, by contrast, points to the congruence noted by Max Weber between the Protestant sectarian and the capitalist ethos, reflected in the presence of a more hardworking, capital-maximizing population south of the border.[73] Canada, as noted earlier, has been less Protestant sectarian than America and, consistent with the Weber thesis, has developed more slowly. The Weberian logic also suggests that Quebec and the American South were economically less advanced because of Catholicism and slavery, and because of the impact of these systems on values and structures.[74] Friedrich Engels, recording his impressions of a brief visit to North America in 1888, emphasized the sharp variation between the "spirit of the Americans" and that of the Canadians. He noted that north of the border, "one imagines that one is in Europe again, and then one thinks that one is in a positively retrogressing and decaying country. Here one sees how necessary the *feverish speculative spirit* of the Americans is for the rapid development of a new country." Engels also pointed to the "economic necessity for an infusion of Yankee blood" for Canada to grow.[75]

The distinctive nature of Canadian society has affected the way her citizens have done business. In analyzing the basis of "a dynamic free enterprise culture," Herschel Hardin argues that

> Greed and hard work and ambition are not enough. . . . It was . . . rough egalitarianism, practical education . . . and the relentless psychic push to keep up in the "Lockian race" that made the exceptional United States go.
>
> But to expect that [in Canada], out of a French Canada tied to its clerical, feudal past, and out of an English-speaking Canada which, although it inherited much of the spirit of liberal capitalism, was nevertheless an elitist, conservative, defensive colony—to expect it *without an intense, ideological revolution*—was to dream a derivative impossibility.[76]

As a result, according to Hardin, Canadian entrepreneurs have been frequently less aggressive, less innovative, and less likely to take risks than American.[77]

Drawing in large part on works by J.J. Brown and Pierre Bourgault, Hardin seeks to demonstrate that private enterprise in Canada "has been a monumental failure" at developing new technology and industry, in that Canadian business has rarely been involved in creating industries to process inventions by Canadians, who have had to go abroad to get their discoveries marketed.[78] The Science Council of Canada, assessing impediments to innovation, emphasizes the "prudence" of Canadians as a major obstacle.[79]

Canadian economist Jerry Podoluk (quoted by Harry Hiller) reports, "investment is a much more significant source of personal income in the United States than in Canada"; and Hiller adds, "Capital investment is necessary for economic development, but the risk involved has generally not appealed to Canadians."[80] Thus, in 1981, investment in stocks amounted to 0.9 percent of the GDP in the United States; the comparable figure for Canada was 0.2 percent.[81] Similarly, in 1985, 20 percent of adult Americans were stockholders, compared to 13 percent of adult Canadians in 1986.[82] Consistent with these findings, the Science Council of Canada has noted that Canadians tend to be savers. As of 1982, the personal savings rate in Canada was 13.7 percent, while the American was 6.5 percent.[83] The Canadian economist Abraham Rotstein contends that "the problem of capital in this country is not that we have too little but, on the contrary, that we have too much."[84]

Taking into consideration the varying sizes of the two populations (ten to one) and per capital GNPs (twelve to one), we may conclude that Canadians invest much more money south of the border than Americans send north, a tendency that has grown greatly over time. Whereas in the early seventies the ratio in absolute terms of American investment in the north to Canadian investment in the south was on the order of five to one, as of 1985 it was three to two.[85] Kenneth Glazier seeks to explain the phenomenon:

> One reason is that Canadians traditionally have been conservative, exhibiting an inferiority complex about their own destiny as a nation and about the potential of their country. . . . President A.H. Ross of Western Decalta Petroleum Ltd., Calgary, in a recent annual report, said that most of Western Decalta's exploration funds are "from foreign sources because the company has not been able to find enough risk capital in Canada."[86]

Glazier thus argues that Canada has suffered, not just from a labor drain and a brain drain, but from a considerable capital drain as well.

Data drawn from opinion polls reinforce these comparative observations about the greater economic prudence of Canadians. This characteristic is reflected, for example, in responses to the question, "If you needed to make a major purchase in the next month, how willing would you be to make that purchase using credit," which was asked in a 1987 survey conducted by Decima and Cambridge Research Incorporated (CRI). Forty-five pecent of Americans replied they would be "very willing" (15 percent were "willing") to use credit, as compared to 34 percent of Canadians (8 percent were "willing"). These differences go back at least to the late sixties, as indicated in the findings of surveys taken in 1968, 1970, and 1979.[87]

Americans are more likely than Canadians to express attitudes that reflect greater absorption of the values of the business-industrial system. The CARA value studies asked a number of questions dealing with feelings about work. The results show that 84 percent of Americans felt "a great deal" of pride in work, as did 77 percent of anglophone Canadians, and 38 percent of francophones; parallel percentages for those saying they never felt exploited were 56, 44, and 37; and for those believing that superiors' instructions should be followed unquestioningly, the percentages were 68, 57, and 45. Americans were least likely to select one of the top three points on a ten-point scale with regard to job satisfaction: 63 percent did, compared with 69 percent of English Canadians, and 74 percent of French Canadians, the most satisfied group overall. This last response pattern, the inverse of those reported for the first three items, may reflect a greater interest among Americans in changing to a better job.

Canadians are somewhat more hostile than Americans to private enterprise. Such sentiments are apparent in responses to surveys conducted in the early eighties by Wright and Myles. When asked to react to the statement, "Corporations benefit owners at the expense of workers and consumers," 67 percent of Canadians agreed, compared to 58 pecent of Americans. Almost half the Americans, 45 percent, compared to 36 percent of their northern neighbors, strongly disagreed with the opinion, "It is possible for a modern society to run effectively without the profit motive." Canadians were more likely to agree that "one of the main reasons for poverty is that the economy is based on private ownership and profits"; 52 percent concurred as opposed to 47 percent of Americans. But this difference is largely the result of Quebec attitudes: 56 percent of Quebeckers agreed, compared to 49 percent of English Canadians.

These national variations are reflected in institutions as well as in attitudes. The famous Fifth Amendment to the United States Constitution not only protects accused persons against self-incrimination, but it and the Fourteenth Amendment provide that persons may not be deprived of "property without due process of law." Hence property holders have a right to be recompensed for government action on the federal or state level that reduces property values or expropriates them. No corresponding rights exist in Canada either in the 1867 or 1982 Constitutions.

The other side of the coin, with respect to the cross-national differences in dealing with the private sector and in economic behavior, is that Canadians have been much more disposed than Americans to call on the state to handle economic and other matters, as the next section indicates.

The Role of Government

The Tory orientation and the smaller population relative to landmass north of the border have meant a larger role for the state in the Canadian economy since Confederation. As of 1982, the proportion of Canadian GNP in government hands was 47.3 percent, compared to 38 percent in the United States.[88] Goldberg and Mercer report that, measured relative to either GDP or GNP, "government spending in Canada is, in proportionate terms, 24.4 per cent greater than in the U.S."[89] If we subtract defense spending—roughly 2 percent for Canada, and 5 to 6 percent for the United States—the gap between the two countries considerably widens.[90]

While there is some government ownership of industry in both countries, it is much more common in Canada. A.J.T. McLeod notes "the frequent appearance of public ownership in Canada," where "the state has always dominated and shaped the . . . economy."[91] Mercer and Goldberg summed up the magnitude of government involvement in the Canadian economy as of 1982:

20

Of 400 top industrial firms, 25 were controlled by the federal or provincial governments. Of the top 50 industrialists, all ranked by sales, 7 were either wholly owned or controlled by the federal or provincial governments. For financial institutions, 9 of the top 25 were federally or provincially owned or controlled. . . .[92]

Although most European states are more involved in economic activities than Canada, the latter "does appear to represent a mid-point between the European and American patterns . . . both in the provision of subsidies to the private sector and in the scope of public enterprise." While below the norm for OECD countries, Canadian subsidies to business and employment in public enterprise were five times the level of those in the United States during the seventies.[93]

Similar variations occur with respect to welfare policies. A detailed comparative analysis of the development of the welfare state in both countries by Robert Kudrle and Theodore Marmor concludes that specific welfare policies have generally been adopted earlier in Canada, and tend to be "more advanced in terms of program development, coverage, and benefits." Seeking to account for these variations, Kudrle and Marmor stress the "ideological difference . . . between Canada and the United States" that "appears to have made a considerable difference in welfare state development. . . . Provincial-federal bargaining mechanisms have often allowed steadier and more advanced policy development once initial jurisdictional problems have been overcome."[94]

Most of the research based on opinion-poll interviews supports this contention. Summarizing surveys of high-level civil servants and federal, state, and provincial legislators, Robert Presthus reports a

sharp difference between the two [national] elites on "economic liberalism," defined as a preference for "big government." . . . Only about 17 per cent of the American legislative elite ranks high on this disposition, compared with fully 40 per cent of their Canadian peers. . . . [T]he direction is the same among bureaucrats, only 17 per cent of whom rank high among the American sample, compared with almost 30 per cent among Canadians.[95]

Differences related to party affiliation in both countries emphasize the cross-national variations. During the 1970s, more Canadian Liberal legislators than American Democrats favored economic liberalism, and more Canadian Conservatives were in favor of it than Republicans. More Conservatives and Republicans in each country tended to disapprove of economic liberalism than Liberals and Democrats, but *Canadian Conservatives approved it more often than American Democrats.*[96]

Other studies provide further evidence of the greater propensity of Canadians to favor a strong role for government. From 1978 to 1979, surveys conducted in the United States and Canada asked respondents to locate themselves on a seven-point scale running from "Government should see to a job and a good standard of living," to "[Government] should let each person get ahead on his own." Not surprisingly, Canadians were much more likely to choose the government-action position, Americans the individualistic response. Fifty-one percent of the latter opted for the three "let-each-person-get-ahead" scale positions, in contrast to 38 percent of their northern neighbors. In 1986, Decima in Canada and CRI in the United States asked respondents to place themselves on an eleven-point scale in reaction to the statement: "The best government is the one which governs the least." As might be expected, those north of the border were much more prone, by 23 to 13 percent, to "totally disagree." Those who indicated any level of disagreement were more likely to be Canadian than American by 42 to 32 percent.

The existence of an electorally viable social-democratic party, the New Democratic Party (NDP), in Canada has been thought by various writers to be an outgrowth of the Tory-statist tradition and stronger collectivity orientation north of the border.[97] However, this thesis has been criticized on the grounds that socialist parties have been weakest in the most traditional parts of Canada: Ontario and New Brunswick.[98] In answer to this line of argument, William Christian and Colin Campbell suggest that the emergence in the sixties and seventies of a social-democratic movement in Quebec, the Parti Québécois, reflects the propensity for the leftist collectivism inherent in Canadian elitist values to appear after the bulwarks of the traditional system break down. They conclude that the development of socialist strength in Quebec is "hardly surprising" since "Quebec's stock of political ideas includes a strong collectivist element. ... Quebec's collectivist past provided receptive and fruitful soil for socialist ideas once the invasion of liberal capitalism had broken the monopoly of the old conservative ideology."[99]

Stratification

Much of the comparative discussion of North America refers implicitly, if not explicitly, to variations in stratification, patterns of class sentiments, hierarchy, and inequality. Reviewing the evidence on the subject, Goldberg and Mercer argue that "Canadians are much more tolerant of ruling elites and oligarchs than Americans."[100] There are two interview-based academic studies dealing with the thesis that Canada is more elitist than the United States that I will mention here: one concerning national variations in value orientations, and one dealing with occupational prestige.

In a study of two communities situated on different sides of the border, Craig Crawford and James Curtis reported that Americans were lower than Canadians on an elite-orientation scale, and higher on achievement orientation.[101] Neil Guppy, a Canadian sociologist, studied the degree of consensus across the social hierarchy with respect to the prestige rankings given to different occupations by cross-national samples. He concluded that "in the United States less emphasis is placed on hierarchical patterns of deference." These findings are congruent with the assumption that there is "stronger class hegemony in Canada," since her privileged classes appear to have more influence over others with respect to evaluations of the worth of occupations.[102]

Cross-national polls conducted over the last fifteen years have sought to estimate support for meritocracy in contrast to equality of result. Their findings point to strong and continuing differences between Americans and Canadians on these issues. Reporting in 1974 on a survey of attitudes of college students in both countries, Milton Rokeach reported that "Canadians are less achievement- and competence-oriented" than Americans, while Canadians, (men, in this case) were "more for equality . . . than their American counterparts."[103]

The CARA-Gallup studies found that Canadians and Americans diverged, as might be expected, when responding to classic statements of conflict between liberty and equality. They were asked:

Which of these two statements comes closest to your own opinion?

A. I find that both freedom and equality are important but if I were to make up my mind for one or the other, I would consider personal freedom more important, that is, everyone can live in freedom and develop without hindrance.

B. Certainly both freedom and equality are important, but if I were to make up my mind for one of the two, I would consider equality more important, that is, that nobody is underprivileged and that social class differences are not so strong.

Most respondents on both sides of the border opted for freedom over equality, but Americans led in this preference. Seventy-two percent agreed with the first statement as compared to 64 percent of the English Canadians and 57 percent of the French Canadians. Conversely, 38 percent of the francophones, 29 percent of the anglophones, and only 20 percent of the Americans said that an emphasis on the reduction of class differences is more important than freedom.

In nations that place the greatest value on individual achievement, we can expect greater concern for equality of opportunity, than with reducing inequality of conditions. Given the stronger achievement orientation south of the border, it is not surprising that Americans have placed more emphasis than Canadians on educational equality as the primary mechanism for social mobility, whereas Canadians have been more engaged in redistributive policies.

In the mid-sixties, the proportion of Canadians aged twenty to twenty-four enrolled in higher-education programs (16 percent) was much lower than that of Americans (32 percent). The educational literature of the time called attention to the more elitist character of the Canadian system, the fact that education in the north was more humanistic and less vocational and professional. The numbers of people attending institutions of higher education have increased greatly in both countries during the past two decades, but there is still a considerable gap. As of 1984, the percentage of that Canadian age cohort (twenty to twenty-four) in all of higher education had risen to 44, but the comparable American figure had increased to 57.[104] Canada not only sharply increased the number of universities and places for students, but her higher-education institutions have incorporated practical and vocationally relevant subjects, expanded the social sciences and graduate programs, and placed greater emphasis on faculty scholarship. Some analysts of changes in Canadian universities have referred to these developments as "Americanizations."[105]

Nevertheless, Canadian elitism still exists, and shows up in the findings that Canada has resembled Britain in recruiting her business and political administrative elites disproportionately from those without a professional or technical education. This point is documented by Wallace Clement in his studies of business leaders, which reveals that Canadians not only have less specialized education than Americans, but also that the former are much more likely to have an elitist social background. As of the mid-seventies, 61 percent of Canadian top executives were of upper-class origin compared to 36 percent of their American colleagues.[106]

Similar results were reported for top civil servants in studies done during the late sixties and seventies.[107] Robert Presthus has argued that the generally more privileged class background of Canadian bureaucrats has reflected "strong traces of the 'generalist,' amateur approach to administration .... Technical aspects of government programmes tend to be de-emphasized, while policy-making and the amateur-classicist syndrome are magnified."[108] Colin Campbell reports that only 29 percent of Canadian bureaucrats he studied, compared with 68 percent of their American counterparts, "cite academic training" as important background for their jobs."[109]

However, as with many other Canadian institutions, the civil service is changing. A survey of bureaucrats in central government agencies by Colin Campbell and George Szablowski in the late seventies finds that "in the past decade Canada has seen a remarkable influx of bureaucrats representing segments of the populace traditionally excluded from senior positions in the public service," and that many of those interviewed had "experienced rapid upward mobility."[110] These developments may reflect the documented decrease in educational inheritance in Canada as the higher-education system has grown.[111] For example, although the proportion of university graduates receiving degrees in business and management has been much greater south of the border than to the north, the gap is slowly declining in proportionate terms: 14 to 5 percent in 1970 to 1971; 24 to 13 percent in 1983.[112]

These findings about attitudes toward stratification and elite behavior are relevant to the cross-national variation in trade-union strength, and to the presence or absence of electorally viable socialist or social-democratic parties noted earlier. While Canada falls behind much of Europe on both items, her trade-union movement has encompassed a significantly larger proportion of the nonagricultural labor force than has the American one for most of the years from 1918 to the present.[113] Furthermore, although the great majority of Canadian and American trade unionists once belonged to the same international unions, the affiliates in the two countries have varied in ways that reflect the diverse national traditions.[114] American social structure and values foster the free market and competitive individualism, an orientation that is not congruent with class consciousness, support for socialist or social-democratic parties, or a strong trade-union movement. Canadian developments, by contrast, have been interpreted as an outgrowth of the influence of the Tory-statist tradition and the stronger collectivity orientation north of the border.[115]

From the mid-thirties to the mid-fifties, union density in the United States grew, temporarily placing the American labor movement ahead of the Canadian in terms of the proportion of the labor force involved. In the same period, the American movement became deeply involved in political action, largely in support of the Democratic party, and adopted political programs calling for a high level of state involvement in planning the economy and sharp increases in welfare and health programs. These developments contrasted with the movement's historic antistatist, syndicalist position. Prior to the thirties, leaders of American workers, both moderate (the American Federation of Labor—AFL) and radical (the Industrial Workers of the World—IWW), opposed a separate labor or socialist party and viewed the state as an enemy.

The changes reflected the impact of the Great Depression, which undermined traditional American beliefs in large sectors of the population, and led to acceptance by a majority of the need for state action to reduce unemployment and assist victims of the economic collapse. As Richard

Hofstadter notes, the depression introduced "a social-democratic tinge" to American party politics that had never before been present.[116] However, this "tinge" declined under the impetus of the postwar economic miracle that, while still reflecting the business cycle, produced a steadily growing economy.

There is evidence from elections results (seven Republican victories in the ten presidential elections held from 1952 on) and the findings of opinion polls that the postwar resurgence gave Americans renewed faith in the promise of their country as an open meritocratic society. Support for statism—nationalization of various industries and socialism in general—declined steeply. A 1975 CRI poll asked respondents how they felt about nationalization of each of eight major industries. In every case, decisive majorities were opposed.[117] Furthermore, the electoral strength of socialist parties in the United States has been below 1 percent in every presidential election held since World War II. Given the evidence of the restoration of faith in traditional American values, it is understandable that support for, and membership in, trade unions have also fallen considerably.

Unlike their American counterparts, Canadian labor officials repeatedly endorsed the principle of independent labor political action from the turn of the century on, and were much more in favor of state intervention.[118] In addition, the effects of the Great Depression and subsequent postwar economic growth on Canada have been quite different. After the Trades and Labour Congress (TLC) and the Canadian Congress of Labour (CCL) merged into the Canadian Labour Congress in the mid-fifties, they joined with the Cooperative Commonwealth Federation (CCF) to form the New Democratic Party (NDP) in 1961. The united Canadian union movement has continued officially to support the NDP.

In contrast to the American experience, the postwar economic boom did not precipitate a return to the values of classical liberalism in Canada because these values never constituted the national tradition north of the border. All Canadian political parties, including the now-governing Tories, remain committed to an activist welfare state, to communitarianism.[119] Furthermore, in spite of improved economic conditions, Canadian socialism has held its own nationally, generally obtaining between fifth and a quarter of the vote in English Canada. The NDP has been the governing or official opposition party in the five provinces west of Quebec. And, as noted, social democracy gained a new bastion in French Canada with the rise of the Parti Québécois to major-party status in the seventies. The Canadian labor movement reached new membership heights in the seventies—close to 40 percent of the employed labor force became members—and the trend continued into the eighties.[120]

This analysis now turns to national unity, to the ways that sub-groups, ethnic and regional, behave in the two societies.

Mosaic and Melting Pot

A major Canadian self-image is that of a mosaic, a society that assures the right to cultural survival to diverse ethnic groups, as compared to the American notion of assimilation into the melting pot. The origin of these differences can be traced to the impact of the Revolution. American universalism, the desire to incorporate diverse groups into one culturally unified whole, is inherent in the country's founding ideology. Canadian particularism—the preservation of subnational group loyalties, as well as the greater independence of the provinces from their federal government than the states from their own—is rooted in the decision of the francophone clerical elite to remain loyal to the British monarchy as a protection against puritanism and democratic populism from across the border. As Canadian sociologist Morton Weinfeld notes,

> The British North America Act of 1867 did not declare the absolute equality of all citizens. Rather, by recognizing certain rights for religious groups (Catholics and Protestants) and linguistic groups (English and French speakers), it legitimated a collectivistic approach to the notion of rights, in contrast to the American emphasis on individual liberties. The binational origin of the Canadian state paved the way for full acceptance of the plural nature of Canadian society.[121]

Most analysts have assumed that industrialization, urbanization, and the spread of education would reduce ethnic and regional consciousness, and that universalism would supplant particularism.[122] However, the validity of these assumptions has been challenged by North American experience. This has been especially so in Canada, where the values underlying the concept of the mosaic meant that various minorities, in addition to the francophones, were able to sustain a stronger group life than comparable ones in the United States.

Canadian ethno-cultural groups have a more protective environment because of the official acceptance of multiculturalism. The country has been formally committed to helping all ethnic groups since the 1969 publication of the fourth volume of the *Report of the Royal Commission on Bilingualism and Biculturalism*. Following this report, in 1971, a multiculturalism policy was instituted, officially designating Canada as a country that is multicultural in a bilingual framework. In a policy announcement to Parliament, the government declared:

we believe that cultural pluralism is the very essence of Canadian identity. Every ethnic group has the right to preserve and develop its own culture and values within the Canadian context. To say we have two official languages is not to say we have two official cultures, and no particular culture is more "official" than another. A policy of multiculturalism must be a policy for all Canadians.[123]

A cabinet ministry was established in 1973 with exclusive responsibility for multiculturalism, and government grants have been directed to the various ethnic minorities for projects designed to celebrate and extend their cultures. Multiculturalism is further protected by being entrenched in the Canadian Constitution; section 27 of the Charter of Rights and Freedoms says "This Charter shall be interpreted in a manner consistent with the preservation and enhancement of the multicultural heritage of Canadians."

The charter explicitly singles out "the Indian, Inuit and Métis people of Canada" for special protection. It guarantees "aboriginal, treaty or other rights or freedoms that pertain to the aboriginal peoples of Canada."[124] Canadian programs for native peoples "include priority in appointments to government jobs, government-built houses at virtually no cost, interest-free loans for equipment . . . and exemptions from hunting restrictions and taxes." And in 1988, Prime Minister Mulroney signed agreements giving northern indigenous peoples title to 260,000 square miles of land. The government has also "promised nearly $1 billion in cash and a voice in the development of an additional 1.1 million square miles of the north."[125] The legal situation of American Indians has also improved, thanks in large measure to the enforcement by the courts of rights guaranteed in old treaties and affirmative-action policies. But the Canadian aboriginal community, larger in size and supported by the values implicit in multiculturalism, have done better in political terms.

The differing organization of Jews in Canada and the United States also shows how the structure and behavior of an ethno-religious group may vary with national environments. The Canadian Jewish community is much better organized than its American counterpart. A single national organization, the Canadian Jewish Congress, represents all Jews in Canada; there is no comparable group in the United States. A much higher proportion of Jewish youth is enrolled in religious day schools in Canada than in the United States, while the intermarriage rate is lower north of the border in spite of the fact that the Jewish community there is much smaller than the American. The community size factor should have led to greater assimilation of Jews in Canada, but the emphasis on particularistic group organization subsumed in the mosaic seemingly helps to perpetuate a more solidaristic Canadian Jewish community.[126]

During the past two decades, blacks have assumed a role within the American polity somewhat like that which the Québécois have played in Canada. The call for "Black Power" has led the United States to accept particularistic standards for dealing with racial and ethnic groups. Much as francophones have legitimated cultural autonomy for other non-Anglo-Saxon Canadians, the changing position of blacks has enabled other American ethnic groups, and women, to claim rights on a group basis. In effect, the United States has moved toward replacing the ideal of the melting pot with that of the mosaic.

Both countries have adopted affirmative-action programs or quotas for minority ethnic and racial groups, and women. The American policy came about through administrative order under President Nixon in 1969, and has been the subject of continued political and judicial controversy. Enforcement of the policy declined during the Reagan administration, and it is subjected to steady, frequently successful, challenge in the courts. In Canada, the Charter of Rights and Freedoms has enshrined the policy in the Constitution, specifically authorizing programs directed to "the amelioration of conditions of disadvantaged individuals or groups including those that are disadvantaged because of race, national or ethnic origin, colour, religion, sex, age or mental or physical disability."[127] As Alan Cairns emphasizes, this provision reflects "a recurring tendency of the Canadian state . . . . [to single] out particular groups or categories for individualized treatment."[128]

If Canada and the United States have reduced some of the variation in the ways they define the position of minorities, they are more disparate than before with respect to the importance of the center and the periphery, the national government versus the regions, states, and provinces. The power of the latter has steadily declined in the United States, but has increased in Canada.[129]

Center and Periphery

Samuel Beer, a leading authority on comparative government, has asserted that political and economic modernization inherently lead to a growth in authority at the center and a decline in state and provincial power, and cites the United States as an example of this process.[130] However, the Canadian experience has not conformed to this trend. As Donald Smiley has effectively pointed out:

> Modernization had led not to centralization in the Canadian federal system but rather to the power, assertiveness, and competence of the provinces. Furthermore, the provinces where modernization

29

has proceeded most rapidly are the most insistent about preserving and extending their autonomy.[131]

The differences between the two countries in this respect show up strikingly in government revenue. While American federal authorities control most of the funds raised and spent by state and local governments, in fiscal terms Canada is a highly decentralized federation: the provinces and municipalities north of the border exceed the federal government in total spending and tax revenue. As of 1985, the federal share of total Canadian tax revenue, not including social-security funds, was 47.6 percent; the equivalent figure for the United States was 56.3 percent.[132]

Canadian provinces have also been more disposed than American states to challenge the power of the federal government. Movements advocating secession have recurred in this century, not only in Quebec, but in part of the Maritimes, the Prairies, and British Columbia as well. The tensions between Ottawa and the provinces and regions are not simply conflicts among politicians over the distribution of power. Public sentiment in Canada remains much more territorial than in the United States. "Unlike the United States where voter turnout falls off precipitously in state elections, turnout in provincial elections historically has paralleled that in Dominion elections."[133] In a comparative analysis of "voting between 1945 and 1970 in seventeen western nations, Canada ranked among the least nationalized," the most diversified regionally, "while the United States was the most nationalized." Three other studies, two dealing with elections in English Canada through this century and the third for all of Canada from 1878 to 1974, each concluded that provincial differences had not declined, or had actually increased over time.[134]

Moreover, the provinces have steadily grown in strength, particularly from the 1960s through to 1987, when the Meech Lake Accord was signed. The opponents of decentralization have found little support in the national tradition. Even a New Democratic Party spokesperson such as Grant Notley, former leader of the Alberta party, have supported a decentralized model of Canada. Arguing against socialist centralizers, Notley emphasizes that regional variations offer Canadian socialists opportunities for experimentation. He argues that "the NDP must recognize that many Canadians do not want to be controlled from Ottawa, that in his home province, the majority of working people, as well as the majority of business men, identify with their provincial government."[135] To accommodate such sentiment, article 38 of the new Constitution allows provinces to opt out of future constitutional amendments if these affect existing provincial powers.[136]

In contrast, federal power in the United States had grown steadily from the Great Depression to the election of Ronald Reagan, and

Reagan has only managed to slow down the trend. Social scientists have been led to ask what has accounted for this discrepancy between the experience of the two countries, to these contradictory developments. Two variables, both of which may be linked to the outcome of the American Revolution, appear to be most important. One is the role of the French Canadians, which was discussed earlier: smaller provinces, seeking to protect their autonomy, have been able to do so because Quebec has always been in the forefront of the struggle. The other is the effect of the difference between the American presidential-congressional system and the British parliamentary model. The greater propensity of Canadian provinces to engage in recurrent struggles with the federal government and to generate third parties may be explained by the fact that regional interests are not nearly as well protected in Parliament as they are in Congress. As I argued more than two decades ago,

> Given the tight national party discipline imposed by a parliamentary as compared with a presidential system, Canadians are forced to find a way of expressing their special regional or other group needs .... The Canadian solution has been to frequently support different parties on a provincial level than those which they back nationally,

so that provincial governments may carry out the representation tasks that in the United States are fulfilled by congressional interest blocs.[137]

The effort to persuade Quebec to accept the 1982 Constitution, which became law without Quebec's agreement, resulted in the 1987 Meech Lake Accord. If ratified, the accord will further expand provincial powers.[138] It includes provisions giving provinces the right to select immigrants, a share in nominating members of the Supreme Court and the Senate, and it requires ratification of constitutional amendments by every province, not seven as at present. It also recognizes Quebec as a "distinct society."

Former Prime Minister Pierre Trudeau contends that the pro vision to allow provinces to stay out of national shared-cost programs if they undertake one "compatible with national objectives," will "enable the provinces to finish off the balkanization of languages and cultures with the balkanization of social services."[139] It is clear that the accord "is a distinct tilt back to a more provincialist conception" of Canada. Those who defend it argue that it gives "little more than symbolic recognition of [the country's] basic sociological, legal and political realities." They note that Quebec *is* in fact a "distinct society," and Canada "a collection of provincial political communities equally as legitimate as the national community."[140]

Without probing more deeply into what are sometimes described as "the murky waters of Meech Lake," I would like simply to note that the accord highlights the unique situation of Canadian federalism and the weak hold that the national state has on her citizens and political leaders. Canada is much more statist than the United States, but its statism is more provincial than federal.

Conclusion

There can be little doubt that, regardless of how much emphasis is placed on structural or cultural (value) factors in accounting for variations, Canada and the United States continue to differ considerably along most of the dimensions suggested in my previous work.[141] Several critics of the cultural approach, such as Arthur K. Davis and Irving Louis Horowitz, have contended that the differences between the two nations have largely been a function of "cultural lag"; that Canada, traditionally somewhat less developed economically than the United States, has been slower to give up the values and lifestyles characteristic of a less industrialized, more agrarian society.[142] Presumably, then, as the structural gap declines, Canada should become more like the United States. This trend should be strengthened by the fact that the "American connection" has resulted in increased domination by American companies over broad sections of Canadian economic life, and that Canada has also become more culturally dependent on the United States through the spread of the American mass media.

Since World War II, substantial changes in economic productivity, in education, and in rates of upward social mobility have indeed reduced the structural gap. But there has been no consistent decline in the pattern of differences in behavior and values. As elaborated in the preceding pages, significant variations remain across the border with respect to a broad range of societal conditions.

The United States has grown more centralized politically, while Canada has moved in the opposite direction. In related fashion, similar lines of political cleavage increasingly cut across all sections south of the border; in the north, regional diversity has increased. Behavioral indicators of Canadian and American economic cultures, with respect to rates of savings or the use of credit, suggest greater, rather than less variation across the border. Differences in class organizational behavior in the two countries, reflected in rates of trade-union membership, have also grown greatly, as have variations in the national party systems, with the growing popularity of the NDP.

Cross-national differences have narrowed in other respects. The due-process rights of the accused are now much stronger in Canada as a result of constitutional changes, but a greater Canadian adherence to the crime control-model nonetheless persists. Furthermore, the large differences in rates of violent crimes have continued. Canada's increased concern with extending equality of opportunity has also helped to make the two societies somewhat more alike with respect to the scope of their educational systems and opportunities to join the elite. Both countries have witnessed an ethnic revival, an increase in particularistic demands by minorities, contributing to a greater acceptance of multiculturalism. The United States, however, continues to be more universalistic in this respect than its neighbor.

Survey data and impressionistic literature continue to support the thesis that Canada is a more elitist society than the United States, although less so than two decades ago. But at the same time, the evidence and logic of analysis suggest that Canadians have grown more supportive than Americans of redistributive equalitarianism. Canadian political parties, including the governing Conservatives, remain committed to an activist welfare state; American parties, particularly the Republicans, have returned to advocacy of a weaker state, one that is less involved in redistributive welfare programs.

The attitudinal evidence indicates that, on most issues, francophone Canadians are at one end, anglophone Canadians in the middle, and Americans at the other end. Quebec, once the most conservative part of Canada, has become the most liberal on social and welare issues. Clearly, as John Porter and others have emphasized, there are particular styles and values that differentiate both Canadian linguistic cultures from the American one.

Their cultural and political differences occasionally cause the two nations some difficulty in understanding each other in the international arena. There are the obvious effects of variations in size, power, and awareness of the other. Canadians object to being taken for granted, and to being ignored by their neighbor. As citizens of a less populous power, they sympathize with small or weak countries that are in conflict with the United States. But beyond the consequences of variations in national power and interests, Canadians and Americans have a somewhat different weltanschauung, or world view. Due to their revolutionary and sectarian Protestant heritages, Americans more than other Western peoples tend to view international politics in nonnegotiable moralistic and ideological terms. Canadians, like Europeans, are more disposed to perceive foreign-policy conflicts as reflections of interest differences, and therefore subject to negotiation and compromise.

Some may argue that I have overemphasized the cultural differences between these two North American democracies, particularly between anglophone Canada and the United States. They may properly point out that the two countries are quite similar to each other when compared to European or other nations. I would not question such a judgment. This is an effort at a detailed comparison of two closely linked neighbors, not of cross-cultural variations on a broad, international scale. As Marcus Cunliffe has well noted, *"narrow comparison brings out dissimilarities, and broad comparison brings out similarities.'*[143]

The United States and Canada remain two nations formed according to different organizing principles. Although some will disagree, there can be no argument. As Margaret Atwood concludes: "Americans and Canadians are not the same; they are the products of two very different histories, two very different situations."[144]

Notes

1. A more comprehensive version of this monograph is forthcoming as a book, *Distinctive Neighbors: The Values and Culture of Canada and the United States.*

2. For a review of findings in the literature see Stephen J. Arnold and James G. Barnes, "Canadian and American National Character as a Basis for Market Segmentation," in Jagdish N. Sheth, ed., *Research in Marketing: A Research Annual,* vol. 2 (Greenwich, Conn.: JAI Press, 1979), esp. 3–6; and Michael A. Goldberg and John Mercer, *The Myth of the North American City: Continentalism Challenged* (Vancouver: University of British Columbia Press, 1986), chap. 10.

3. By culture I mean, in Clifford Geertz's words, "a historically transmitted pattern of meanings embodied in symbols, a system of inherited conceptions expressed in symbolic forms by means of which men communicate, perpetuate, and develop their knowledge about and attitudes toward life." Clifford Geertz, *The Interpretation of Cultures: Selected Essays by Clifford Geertz* (New York: Basic Books, 1973), 89.

4. My initial treatment of this subject was presented in my book, *The First New Nation: The United States in Historical and Comparative Perspective* (New York: Basic Books, 1963), esp. chap. 7. It was elaborated in Seymour Martin Lipset, "Revolution and Counter-Revolution—The United States and Canada," in *The Revolutionary Theme in Contemporary America,* ed. Thomas R. Ford (Lexington: University of Kentucky Press, 1965). My more recent work includes "Revolution and Counter-Revolution: Some Comments at a Conference Analyzing the Bicentennial of a Celebrated North American Divorce," in *Perspectives on Evolution and Revolution,* ed. Richard A. Preston, Duke University Center for Commonwealth and Comparative Studies Series, no. 46 (Durham: Duke University Press, 1979); "Canada and the United States: The Cultural Dimension," in *Canada and the United States: Enduring Friendship, Persistent Stress,* ed. Charles F. Doran and John M. Sigler (Englewood Cliffs, N.J.: Prentice-Hall, 1985); "Historical Traditions and National Characteristics: A Comparative Analysis of Canada and the United States," *Canadian Journal of Sociology* 11 (Summer 1986).

5. Louis Hartz, *The Founding of New Societies: Studies in the History of the United States, Latin America, South Africa, Canada, and Australia* (New York: Harcourt, Brace and World, 1964), 1–48.

6. *Ibid.,* 34.

7. Robin W. Winks, *The Relevance of Canadian History: U.S. and Imperial Perspectives* (Toronto: Macmillan Canada, 1979), xiii–xiv.

8. Northrop Frye, *Divisions on a Ground: Essays on Canadian Culture,* ed. James Polk (Toronto: House of Anansi Press, 1982), 66.

9. See S.D. Clark, *Movements of Political Protest in Canada, 1640-1840,* Social Credit in Alberta: Its Background and Development, no. 9 (Toronto: University of Toronto Press, 1959); and *Canadian Society in Historical Perspective,* McGraw-Hill Ryerson Series in Canadian Sociology (Toronto: McGraw-Hill Ryerson, 1976); Frank H. Underhill, *In Search of Canadian Liberalism* (Toronto: Macmillan Canada, 1960); Arthur R.M. Lower, *Colony to Nation* (1946; reprint, Don Mills, Ont.: Longmans, 1964); George Grant, *Lament for a Nation: The Defeat of Canadian Nationalism* (Princeton: D. Van Nostrand, 1965); and John Porter, *The Vertical Mosaic: An Analysis of Social Class and Power in Canada,* Studies in the Structure of Power: Decision-Making in Canada, no. 2 (Toronto: University of Toronto Press, 1965).

10. Underhill, *In Search,* 222.

11. William A. Stahl, " 'May He Have Dominion . . .' ": Civil Religion and the Legitimation of Canadian Confederation" (Luther College, University of Regina, 1986), 4.

12. Reg Whitaker, "Images of the State in Canada," in *The Canadian State: Political Economy and Political Power,* ed. Leo Panitch (Toronto: University of Toronto Press, 1977), 38.

13. Louis Hartz, *The Liberal Tradition in America: An Interpretation of American Political Thought Since the Revolution* (New York: Harcourt, Brace and World, 1955); Gad Horowitz, "Notes on 'Conservatism, Liberalism and Socialism in Canada,' " *Canadian Journal of Political Science* 11 (June 1978): 390.

14. Gad Horowitz, "Tories, Socialists and the Demise of Canada," *Canadian Dimension* 2, no. 4 (May-June 1965): 2. See also his *Canadian Labour in Politics,* Studies in the Structure of Power: Decision-Making in Canada, no. 4 (Toronto: University of Toronto Press, 1968), chap. 1.

15. James Bryce, *Modern Democracies,* vol. 1, (New York: Macmillan, 1921), chap. 34.

16. S.D. Clark, *The Developing Canadian Community* (Toronto: University of Toronto Press, 1962), 188-9. See also Harold A. Innis, "Transportation as a Factor in Canadian Economic History," "Government Ownership and the Canadian Scene," "An Introduction to Canadian Economic Studies," "Significant Factors in Canadian Economic Development," in *Essays in Canadian Economic History,* ed. Mary Q. Innis (Toronto: University of Toronto Press, 1956); Harold A. Innis, *The Fur Trade in Canada: An Introduction to Canadian Economic History* (New Haven: Yale University Press, 1962); Donald Creighton, *The Empire of the St. Lawrence* (Toronto: Macmillan Canada, 1956). For evaluation see J.T. McLeod, "The Free Enterprise Dodo is No Phoenix," *The Canadian Forum* 56, no. 663 (August 1976).

17. Edgar W. McInnis, *The Unguarded Frontier: A History of American-Canadian Relations* (Garden City, N.J.: Doubleday, Doran, 1942), 306-7.

18. See, for example, H. Blair Neatby, *The Politics of Chaos: Canada in the Thirties* (Toronto: Macmillan Canada, 1972), 10.

19. John Charles Weaver, "Imperilled Dreams: Canadian Opposition to the American Empire, 1918-1930" (Ph.D. diss., Duke University, 1973).

20. For a statement by Canada's foremost contemporary conservative philosopher on the differences between American and Canadian conservatism see Grant, *Lament for a Nation,* 64-65; 70-71. See also Charles Taylor, *Radical Tories: The Conservative Tradition in Canada* (Toronto: House of Anansi Press, 1982).

21. Richard Gwyn, *The 49th Paradox: Canada in North America* (Toronto: McClelland and Stewart, 1985), 11.

22. Innis, "Great Britain, the United States and Canada," in *Essays,* 406.

23. Frye, *Divisions on a Ground,* 46.

24. Margaret Atwood, *Survival: A Thematic Guide to Canadian Literature* (Toronto: House of Anansi Press, 1972) 31, 32, 33.

25. *Ibid.,* 171.

26. *Ibid.,* 131.

27. Russell M. Brown, "Telemachus and Oedipus: Images and Authority in Canadian and American Fiction" (University of Toronto, n.d.), 2.

28. *Ibid.,* 5-6.

29. *Ibid.,* 7.

30. *Ibid.,* 8.

31. Mary Jean Green, "Writing in a Motherland" (Dartmouth College, 1984).

32. Hugh MacLennan, "A Society in Revolt," in *Voices of Canada: An Introduction to Canadian Culture,* ed. Judith Webster (Burlington, Vt.: Association for Canadian Studies in the United States, 1977), 30.

33. Scott Symons, "The Canadian Bestiary: Ongoing Literary Depravity," *West Coast Review* 11, no. 3 (Jan. 1977): 14.

34. Atwood, *Survival,* 34.

35. "Beautiful Losers of 1985," *Saturday Night* 101 (Jan. 1986): 25.

36. Robert Fothergill, "Coward, Bully or Clown: The Dream-Life of a Younger Brother," in *Canadian Film Reader,* ed. Seth Feldman and Joyce Nelson, Take One Film Book Series, no. 5 (Toronto: Peter Martin Associates, 1977), 242, 243.

37. Geoff Pevere, "Images of Men," *Canadian Forum* 64, no. 746 (February 1985): 24, 28.

38. Ronald Sutherland, *The New Hero: Essays in Comparative Québec/Canadian Literature* (Toronto: Macmillan Canada, 1977), 16; A.J.M. Smith, "Evolution and Revolution as Aspects of English-Canadian and American Literature," in *Perspectives,* ed. Preston, 213.

39. Innis, "The Church in Canada," in *Essays,* 385.

40. The Anglican church has declined greatly in modern times, as the

ecumencial United church has emerged as the largest Protestant denomination.

41. John Webster Grant, " 'At Least You Knew Where You Stood With Them': Reflections on Religious Pluralism in Canada and the United States," *Studies in Religion: Sciences Religieuses* 2 (Spring 1973): 341.

42. Samuel Delbert Clark, "The Canadian Community," in *Canada,* ed. George W. Brown, The United Nations Series (Berkeley: University of California Press, 1950), 388.

43. Rodney Stark and William Sims Bainbridge, *The Future of Religion: Secularization, Revival and Cult Formation* (Berkeley: University of California Press, 1985), 461.

44. Edmund Burke, *Burke's Politics: Selected Writings and Speeches of Edmund Burke on Reform, Revolution, and War,* ed. Ross J.S. Hoffman and Paul Levack (1949; reprint, New York: Alfred A. Knopf, Borzoi, 1967), 71.

45. Alexis de Tocqueville, *Democracy in America,* new ed., vol. 1, trans. Henry Reeve (London: Longmans, Green, 1889), 312-19.

46. Kenneth Westhues, "Stars and Stripes, the Maple Leaf, and the Papal Coat of Arms," *Canadian Journal of Sociology: Cahiers canadiens de sociologie* 3 (Spring 1978): 251.

47. See R.L. Bruckberger, "The American Catholics as a Minority," in *Roman Catholicism and the American Way of Life,* ed. Thomas T. McAvoy (Notre Dame: University of Notre Dame Press, 1960), 45-47.

48. Westhues, "Stars and Stripes," 256.

49. Harold Fallding, "Mainline Protestantism in Canada and the United States of America: An Overview," *Canadian Journal of Sociology: Cahiers canadiens de sociologie* 3 (Spring 1978): 145. See also Reginald W. Bibby, "Religious Encasement in Canada: An Argument for Protestant and Catholic Entrenchment," *Social Compass* 32 (1985).

50. Harry H. Hiller, "Continentalism and the Third Force in Religion," *Canadian Journal of Sociology: Cahiers canadiens de sociologie* 3 (Spring 1978): 192.

51. Reginald W. Bibby, *Fragmented Gods: The Poverty and Potential of Religion in Canada* (Toronto: Irwin Publishing, 1987), 219.

52. See CARA (Center for Applied Research in the Apostolate), *Values Study of Canada* (Washington, D.C.: May 1983). The percentages for the United States are based on 1,729 respondents, and for Canada, on 1,251 respondents (338 francophone and 913 anglophone).

53. Canadian Conference of Catholic Bishops, "A Statement on Social Policy," *Dissent* (Summer 1988). See also Gregory Baum and Duncan Cameron, *Ethics and Economics: Canada's Catholic Bishops on the Economic Crisis,* The Canadian Issues Series (Toronto: James Lorimer, 1984).

54. John F. Burns, "Canadian Church Approves Homosexual Ministers," *New York Times*, 28 Aug. 1988, late edition.

55. These models are taken from the work of Herbert L. Packer, "Two Models of the Criminal Process," *University of Pennsylvania Law Review* 113 (Nov. 1964). See also John Hagan and Jeffrey Leon, "Philosophy and Sociology of Crime Control," in *Social System and Legal Process,* ed. Harry M. Johnson (San Francisco: Jossey-Bass, 1978), 182.

56. Robert K. Merton, *Social Theory and Social Structure,* rev. and enl. ed. (1949; reprint, Glencoe, Ill.: The Free Press, 1957), 169.

57. For data on the two countries, see Dane Archer and Rosemary Gartner, "Comparative Crime Data File: Nations," in *Violence and Crime in Cross-National Perspective* (New Haven: Yale University Press, 1984), appendix.

58. Al Neuharth, "Giant, Genteel Neighbor," *USA Today,* 26 Aug. 1988. There is, however, much less difference between the two with respect to crimes involving property, for example, theft and burglary. For detailed comparative statistics from the mid-1960s to the mid-1970s see Alex C. Michalos, *Crime, Justice, and Politics,* vol. 2 of *North American Social Report: A Comparative Study of the Quality of Life in Canada and the USA from 1964 to 1974* (Boston: D. Reidel, 1980), 74-150; John Hagan, *The Disreputable Pleasures,* McGraw-Hill Ryerson Series in Canadian Sociology (Toronto: McGraw-Hill Ryerson, 1977), 48-54; and Louise I. Shelley, "American Crime: An International Anomaly?," *Comparative Social Research* 8 (1985).

59. See Charles Lewis Taylor and David A. Jodice, *Political Protest and Government Change,* vol. 2 of *World Handbook of Political and Social Indicators,* 3d ed. (New Haven: Yale University Press, 1983), 19-25, 33-36, 47-51.

60. There was no significant difference between the two Canadian linguistic groups on this item.

61. Ted E. Thomas, "The Gun Control Issue: A Sociological Analysis of United States and Canadian Attitudes and Policies" (Mills College, 1983), 40. For a comprehensive report see Elisabeth Scarff, *Evaluation of the Canadian Gun Control Legislation: Final Report* (Ottawa: Minister of Supply and Services Canada, 1983).

62. There was no difference in the attitudes of the two Canadian linguistic groups on this issue.

63. David R. Francis, "Why Canada is Safer than US," *Christian Science Monitor,* 2 Jan. 1987.

64. F.L. Morton and Leslie A. Pal, "The Impact of the Charter of Rights on Public Administration," *Canadian Public Administration: Administration publique du Canada* 28 (Summer 1985), 241.

65. Edgar Z. Friedenberg, "Culture in Canadian Context," in *An Introduction to Sociology,* ed. M. Michael Rosenberg et al. (Toronto: Methuen, 1983), 128.

66. Robert A. Sedler, "Constitutional Protection of Individual Rights in Canada: The Impact of the New Canadian Charter of Rights and Freedoms," *Notre Dame Law Review* 59 (1983-84): 1217.

67. John Mercer and Michael Goldberg, "Value Differences and Their Meaning for Urban Development in the U.S.A.," UBC Research in Land Economics, Working Paper, no. 12 (Vancouver: Faculty of Commerce, University of British Columbia, 1982), 22.

68. Paul C. Weiler, "The Evolution of the Charter: A View From the Outside," in *Litigating the Values of a Nation: The Canadian Charter of Rights and Freedoms,* ed. Joseph M. Weiler and Robin M. Elliot (Toronto: Carswell, 1986), 52, 53, 57; see also Dale Gibson, "Reasonable Limits Under the Canadian Charter of Rights and Freedoms," *Manitoba Law Journal* 15, no. 1 (1985).

69. Anne F. Bayefsky, "The Judicial Function Under the Canadian Charter of Rights and Freedoms," *McGill Law Journal* 32 (1986-87): 817-18; and Edward McWhinney, *Canada and the Constitution, 1979-1982: Patriation and the Charter of Rights* (Toronto: University of Toronto Press, 1982), chap. 6.

70. José Woehrling, "Minority Cultural and Linguistic Rights and Equality Rights in the Canadian Charter of Rights and Freedoms," *McGill Law Journal* 31 (1985-86): 89.

71. *Ibid.,* 90.

72. "The Italian Economy: Living with Instability," *The Economist* 306 (27 Feb.-4 Mar. 1988): survey 9. The data are from OECD.

73. Max Weber, *The Protestant Ethic and the Spirit of Capitalism,* trans. Talcott Parsons (1930; reprint, New York: Charles Scribner's Sons, 1958).

74. For a discussion of past variations between English and French Canada, see Seymour Martin Lipset, "Values, Education, and Entrepreneurship," in *Elites in Latin America*, ed. Lipset and Aldo Solari (New York: Oxford University Press, 1967), 11-12.

75. Friedrich Engels to Sorge, 10 Sept. 1888, *Letters to Americans,* Karl Marx and Friedrich Engels (New York: International, 1953), 204. Emphasis added.

76. Herschel Hardin, *A Nation Unaware: The Canadian Economic Culture* (Vancouver: J.J. Douglas, 1974), 62.

77. Peter Karl Kresl also makes this point. See his "An Economics Perspective: Canada in the International Economy," in *Understanding Canada: A Multidisciplinary Introduction to Canadian Studies,* ed. William Metcalfe (New York: New York University Press, 1982), 240.

78. See J.J. Brown, *Ideas in Exile: A History of Canadian Invention* (Toronto: McClelland and Stewart, 1967); and Pierre L. Bougault, *Innovation and the Structure of Canadian Industry,* The Science Council of Canada Special Study, no. 23 (Ottawa: Information Canada, 1972); Hardin, *A Nation Unaware,* 102-5.

79. Science Council of Canada, "Innovation in a Cold Climate: 'Impediments to Innovation,'" in *Independence: The Canadian Challenge,* ed. Abraham Rotstein and Gary Lax (Toronto: The Committee for an Independent Canada, 1972), 123-24. Similar conclusions were reached in a 1988 government report. See David Spurgeon, "A Psychiatrist Crusades to Bring Risk Taking to Canadian Science," *Scientist* (11 July 1988): 2.

80. Harry H. Hiller, *Canadian Society: A Sociological Analysis* (Scarborough, Ont.; Prentice-Hall Canada, 1976), 144.

81. *Japan 1983: An International Comparison* (Tokyo: Keizzi Koho Center, 1983), 8. The source for this is the United Nations *Monthly Bulletin of Statistics,* July 1983.

82. Robert Sexty, "Canadian Business: Who Owns It? Who Controls It? Who Cares?" (Memorial University of Newfoundland, 1988); *New York Stock Exchange Fact Book* (New York: New York Stock Exchange, 1987), 58.

83. Directorate of Intelligence, *Handbook of Economic Statistics, 1983* (Washington, D.C.: Central Intelligence Agency, 1983), 58. See also Janet Jarrett, "Why Canadians Save More than Americans," *The Canadian Business Review* 7, no. 3 (Autumn 1980): 37.

84. Abraham Rotstein, "Repairing the Fences," *Canadian Forum* 64, no. 747 (March 1985): 14.

85. Alan M. Rugman, *Outward Bound: Canadian Direct Investment in the United States* (Washington, D.C. and Toronto: Canadian-American Committee, 1987), 3-6.

86. Kenneth M. Glazier, "Canadian Investment in the United States: 'Putting Your Money Where Your Mouth Is,'" *Journal of Contemporary Business* 1, no. 4 (Autumn 1972): 61. R.T. Naylor has noted similar trends in the pre-World War I period. See his *Industrial Development,* vol. 2 of *The History of Canadian Business, 1867-1914* (Toronto: James Lorimer, 1975), 241.

87. See Stephen J. Arnold and Douglas J. Tigert, "Canadians and Americans: A Comparative Analysis," *International Journal of Comparative Sociology* 15 (Mar.-June 1974); and Stephen J. Arnold and James G. Barnes, "Canadians and Americans: Implications for

Marketing," in *Problems in Canadian Marketing,* ed. Donald N. Thompson (Chicago: American Marketing Association, 1977).

88. Goldberg and Mercer, *Myth,* 100, table 4-6. Five years later the figures were 47 percent (Canada) to 37 percent (the United States). Pierre Lemieux, "Will Canada's Tax Reform Have a Supply-Side Effect?," *Wall Street Journal,* 2 Sept. 1988, Eastern edition.

89. Goldberg and Mercer, *Myth,* 85.

90. See *World Military Expenditures and Arms Transfers, 1971-1980* (Washington, D.C.: U.S. Arms Control and Disarmament Agency, 1982), 42, 71.

91. McLeod, "The Free Enterprise Dodo," 9, 6. See also Hugh G.J. Aitken, "Defensive Expansionism: The State and Economic Growth in Canada," in *The State and Economic Growth,* ed. Aitken (New York: Social Science Research Council, 1959); and H.V. Nelles, "Defensive Expansionism Revisited: Federalism, the State and Economic Nationalism in Canada, 1959-1979," *The (Japanese) Annual Review of Canadian Studies* 2 (1980).

92. Mercer and Goldberg, "Value Differences," 27.

93. Keith G. Banting, "Images of the Modern State: An Introduction," in *State and Society: Canada in Comparative Perspective,* ed. Banting, The Collected Research Studies, Royal Commission on the Economic Union and Development Prospects for Canada, no. 31 (Toronto: University of Toronto Press, 1986), 3-4.

94. Robert T. Kudrle and Theodore R. Marmor, "The Development of Welfare States in North America," in *The Development of Welfare States in Europe and America,* ed. Peter Flora and Arnold J. Heidenheimer (New Brunswick, N.J.: Transaction Books, 1981), 110, 111. Also, "ideological difference" is defined as Canadians being "more supportive to the notion of state action for national and provincial development" than are Americans (89).

95. Robert Presthus, *Elites in the Policy Process* (London: Cambridge University Press, 1974), 463.

96. Robert Presthus, "Aspects of Political Culture and Legislative Behavior: United States and Canada," in *Cross-National Perspectives:*

United States and Canada, ed. Presthus, vol. 24 of *International Studies in Sociology and Social Anthropology* (Leiden, Netherlands: E.J. Brill, 1977), 15.

97. See Hartz, *Liberal Tradition* and *Founding,* 1–48; Horowitz, *Canadian Labour,* chap. 1; and Seymour Martin Lipset, "Why No Socialism in the United States?," in *Sources of Contemporary Radicalism,* ed. Seweyrn Bialer and Sophia Sluzar, vol. 1 of *Radicalism in the Contemporary Age,* Studies of the Research Institute on International Change, Columbia University (Boulder: Westview Press, 1977), 79–83.

98. See Robert J. Brym, "Social Movements and Third Parties," in *Models and Myths in Canadian Sociology,* ed. S.D. Berkowitz (Toronto: Butterworths, 1984), 34–35.

99. William Christian and Colin Campbell, *Political Parties and Ideologies in Canada: Liberals, Conservatives, Socialists, Nationalists,* 2d ed., McGraw-Hill Ryerson Series in Canadian Politics (Toronto: McGraw-Hill Ryerson, 1983), 36.

100. Goldberg and Mercer, *Myth,* 247.

101. Craig Crawford and James Curtis, "English Canadian—American Differences in Value Orientations: Survey Comparisons Bearing on Lipset's Thesis," *Studies in Comparative International Development* 14, nos. 3–4 (Fall-Winter 1979): 32–33.

102. L. Neil Guppy, "Dissensus or Consensus: A Cross-National Comparison of Occupational Prestige Scales," *Canadian Journal of Sociology: Cahiers canadiens de sociologie* 9 (Winter 1984): 79–80.

103. M. Rokeach, "Some Reflections about the Place of Values in Canadian Social Science," in *Perspectives on the Social Sciences in Canada,* ed. T.N. Guinsburg and G.L. Reuber (Toronto: University of Toronto Press, 1974), 164.

104. World Bank, *World Development Report, 1987* (New York: Oxford University Press, 1987), 263.

105. Claude Bissell, "The Place of Learning and the Arts in Canadian Life," in *Perspectives,* ed. Preston, 198.

106. Wallace Clement, "The Economic Elite in Canada and the United

States: 2. Corporate, Ascriptive, and Social Characteristics," in *Continental Corporate Power: Economic Elite Linkages between Canada and the United States* (Toronto: McClelland and Stewart, 1977). See also A.E. Safarian, *The Performance of Foreign-Owned Firms in Canada* (Washington, D.C. and Montreal: Canadian-American Committee, 1969), 13.

107. Robert Presthus and William V. Monopoli, "Bureaucracy in the United States and Canada: Social, Attitudinal, and Behavioral Variables," in *Cross-National Perspectives,* ed. Presthus; Colin Campbell, *Governments Under Stress: Political Executives and Key Bureaucrats in Washington, London, and Ottawa* (Toronto: University of Toronto Press, 1983).

108. Robert Presthus, *Elite Accommodation in Canadian Politics* (Toronto: Macmillan Canada, 1973), 34.

109. Campbell, *Governments,* 314.

110. Colin Campbell and George J. Szablowski, *The Superbureaucrats: Structure and Behaviour in Central Agencies* (Toronto: Macmillan Canada, 1979), 105, 121.

111. Ronald Manzer, *Canada: A Socio-Political Report,* McGraw-Hill Ryerson Series in Canadian Politics (Toronto: McGraw-Hill Ryerson, 1974), 188-206.

112. Robert M. Pike, "Education and the Schools," in *Understanding Canadian Society,* ed. James Curtis and Lorne Tepperman (Toronto: McGraw-Hill Ryerson, 1988), 276-77.

113. S.M. Lipset, "North American Labor Movements: A Comparative Perspective," in *Unions in Transition: Entering the Second Century,* ed. Lipset (San Francisco: Institute for Contemporary Studies, 1986), 421-77.

114. For a general historical analysis of the tensions between the two since the formation of the AFL, see Robert H. Babcock, *Gompers in Canada: A Study in American Continentalism Before the First World War* (Toronto: University of Toronto Press, 1974).

115. For an earlier effort to account for a socialist party in Canada and the absence of one in the United States, see Seymour Martin Lipset,

"Radicalism in North America: A Comparative View of the Party Systems in Canada and the United States," in *Transactions of the Royal Society of Canada: Mémoires de la Société royale du Canada,* 4th ser., no. 16 (1976). In that paper, I emphasize the role of diverse electoral and constitutional structures in facilitating a multiparty system in Canada and a two-party one in the United States. Analyzing the reasons for greater union density in Canada has convinced me that the emphasis in the 1976 paper was wrong; that political cultural values are more important.

116. Richard Hofstadter, *The Age of Reform: From Bryan to F.D.R.* (1955; reprint, New York: Alfred A. Knopf, Borzoi, 1969), 306.

117. See Seymour Martin Lipset and William Schneider, *The Confidence Gap: Business, Labor, and Government in the Public Mind,* rev. ed. (Baltimore: Johns Hopkins University Press, 1987), 285-87.

118. See Charles Lipton, *The Trade Union Movement of Canada, 1827-1959* (1967; reprint, Toronto: NC Press, 1973), 75-76, 118-21, and 233-36; Harold A. Logan, *The History of Trade-Union Organization in Canada* (Chicago: University of Chicago Press, 1928), 245-48.

119. During the Manitoba provincial election campaign in March 1986, the leader of the Conservative opposition to the incumbent NDP, Gary Filmon, told an American reporter that he decided not to campaign against socialism because "the talk of socialism doesn't seem to have a sting" in Canada. In fact, he accused "the socialist government of 'neglecting' and 'starving' Manitoba's elaborate health and welfare system." He promised to restore services cut by the NDP. Herbert N. Denton, "Socialists Seek Reelection in Manitoba," *Washington Post,* 18 Mar. 1986, sec. A.

120. The cross-national differences in union strength are not a function of structural variations in the two economies. For a detailed analysis see Lipset, "North American Labor Movements."

121. Morton Weinfeld, "Canadian Jews and Canadian Pluralism," in *American Pluralism and the Jewish Community,* ed. S.M. Lipset (forthcoming).

122. Nathan Glazer and Daniel Patrick Moynihan, *Beyond the Melting Pot: The Negros, Puerto Ricans, Jews, Italians, and Irish of New York City,* Publications of the Joint Center for Urban Studies of the

Massachusetts Institute of Technology and Harvard University (Cambridge: M.I.T. Press and Harvard University Press, 1963), 6-7.

123. Canada, *House of Commons Debates: Official Report,* vol. 8 (13 Sept.-19 Oct. 1971), 8580-81. Many francophones have preferred a two-cultures model, seeing in multiculturalism a way of denying the French in Canada equal status with the English. Richard Simeon and David J. Elkins, "Conclusion: Province, Nation, Country and Confederation," in *Small Worlds: Provinces and Parties in Canadian Political Life,* ed. Elkins and Simeon (Toronto: Methuen, 1980), 287.

124. Alan Cairns, "The Embedded State: State-Society Relations in Canada," in *State and Society,* ed. Banting, 66.

125. John F. Burns, "Canada Tries to Make Restitution to Its Own," *New York Times,* Sunday, 11 Sept. 1988, late ed., sec. E.

126. Stuart Schoenfeld, "The Jewish Religion in North America: Canadian and American Comparisons," *Canadian Journal of Sociology: Cahiers canadiens de sociologie,* 3 (Spring 1978). For an update and elaboration, see Weinfeld, "Canadian Jews."

127. Cairns, "Embedded State," 66.

128. *Ibid.,* 67.

129. See Mildred A. Schwartz, *Politics and Territory: The Sociology of Regional Persistence in Canada* (Montreal: McGill-Queen's University Press, 1974).

130. Samuel H. Beer, "The Modernization of American Federalism," *Publius* 3, no. 2 (Fall 1973), 52. See John Porter, *The Measure of Canadian Society: Education, Equality and Opportunity,* Carleton Library Series, no. 144 (Ottawa: Carleton University Press, 1987) 172-73, for an argument that a decentralized federal system such as Canada's runs against the current of modernization.

131. Donald V. Smiley, "Public Sector Politics, Modernization and Federalism: The Canadian and American Experiences," *Publius* 14, no. 1 (Winter 1984), 59. For a comprehensive discussion of the factors making for centralization and decentralization, see Richard Simeon,

"Considerations on Centralization and Decentralization," *Canadian Public Administration: Administration publique du Canada* 29 (Autumn 1986).

132. Cairns, "Embedded State," 59-60; and *Statistiques de recettes publiques des pays membres de l'OCDE: Revenue Statistics of OECD Member Countries, 1965-1986* (Paris: Organization for Economic Co-operation and Development, 1987), 213, 232.

133. William Mishler, *Political Participation in Canada: Prospects for Democratic Citizenship*, Canadian Controversies Series (Toronto: Macmillan Canada, 1979), 31.

134. Roger Gibbins, *Regionalism: Territorial Politics in Canada and the United States* (Toronto: Butterworths, 1982), 158. This book is an excellent detailed analysis of the greater emphasis on territorial, regional politics in Canada than in the United States. See also Richard Johnston, "Federal and Provincial Voting: Contemporary Patterns and Historical Evolution," in *Small Worlds,* ed. Elkins and Simeon, 172, for documentation that "Canadian politics are becoming less national and more provincial."

135. Grant Notley, "Comments," in *Canada, What's Left? A New Social Contract Pro and Con,* ed. John Richards and Don Kerr (Edmonton: NeWest Press, 1986), 154-55. Alan Blakeney has voiced a similar position. See his "Decentralization: A Qualified Defense," in *Canada,* ed. Richards and Kerr, 147-52.

136. Ivo D. Duchacek, "Consociational Cradle of Federalism," *Publius* 15, no. 2 (Spring 1985), 41.

137. Lipset, "Radicalism," 47.

138. For a comprehensive discussion, see the articles in the special supplement on the Meech Lake Accord, *Canadian Public Policy: Analyse de politiques* 14 (Sept. 1988).

139. Mary Janigan, "Trudeau's Power Punch," *Maclean's* 100 (8 June 1987), 10.

140. Richard Simeon, "Meech Lake and Shifting Conceptions of Canadian Federalism," *Canadian Public Policy: Analyse de politiques* 14 (Sept. 1988), S15, S12, S14.

141. Theoretical reconsiderations and examination of more recent events and data have led me to modify some earlier generalizations, for example, by recognizing that implicit in greater elitism is a higher level of support for equality of result.

142. Arthur K. Davis, "Canadian Society and History as Hinterland Versus Metropolis," in *Canadian Society: Pluralism, Change, and Conflict,* ed. Richard J. Ossenberg (Scarborough, Ont.: Prentice-Hall, 1971); and Irving Louis Horowitz, "The Hemispheric Connection: A Critique and Corrective to the Entrepreneurial Thesis of Development with Special Emphasis on the Canadian Case," *Queen's Quarterly* 80 (Autumn 1973).

143. Marcus Cunliffe, "New World, Old World: The Historical Antithesis," in *Lessons From America*, ed. Richard Rose (London: Macmillan, 1974), 45.

144. Margaret Atwood, *Second Words: Selected Critical Prose* (Toronto: House of Anansi Press, 1982), 392.

The Borderlands Monograph Series has published:

1. Borderlands Reflections: The United States and Canada.
   Lauren McKinsey and Victor Konrad
2. Canada as a Borderlands Society.
   Roger Gibbins
3. North American Cultures: Values and Institutions in Canada and the United States.
   Seymour Martin Lipset

BORDERLANDS